THE SPRINGBURN EXPERIENCE

AN ORAL HISTORY OF WORK IN A RAILWAY COMMUNITY
FROM 1840 TO THE PRESENT DAY

THE SPRINGBURN EXPERIENCE

AN ORAL HISTORY OF WORK IN A RAILWAY COMMUNITY
FROM 1840 TO THE PRESENT DAY

Gerard Hutchison & Mark O'Neill

Polygon *living memory*

EDINBURGH

© Gerard Hutchison and Mark O'Neill 1989

Polygon
22 George Square, Edinburgh

Set in Century Schoolbook
by the Alden Press, London
and printed in Great Britain by
Bell and Bain Ltd., Glasgow

British Library Cataloguing
  in publication data
Hutchison, Gerard
    The Springburn experience: an oral history of work
    in a railway community from 1840 to the present day.—
    (Living memory)
    1. Scotland. Strathclyde Region. Glasgow.
    Springburn. Railway engineering industries.
    Biographies collections
    I. Title II. O'Neill, Mark III. Series
    338.47′6521′00922

ISBN 0 7486 6008 9

CONTENTS

FOREWORD
by Campbell Christie
Page vi

INTRODUCTION & ACKNOWLEDGEMENTS
Page viii

BIBLIOGRAPHY
Page xiv

———————— CHAPTER 1 ————————

The Nineteenth Century Legacy
Page 2

———————— CHAPTER 2 ————————

Workers' Organisations:
Co-operatives & Trade Unions
Page 22

———————— CHAPTER 3 ————————

Apprenticeship:
The Door to a Job for Life
Page 42

———————— CHAPTER 4 ————————

Health & Safety
Page 56

———————— CHAPTER 5 ————————

War Work & Women
Page 68

———————— CHAPTER 6 ————————

Unemployment
Page 80

WORK IN THE 80s
Page 90

FOREWORD

For me, Springburn will always be full of people and full of excitement. My memories are of thousands of men jumping on and off trams or tramping up or down Springburn Road during week-day mornings and evenings to and from one of the four great railway works at Cowlairs, Hyde Park, the Caley or the Atlas Works. Of thousands of women and children filling Springburn Road on Saturday mornings, shopping in the hundreds of shops which lined the street for the mile or so from Petershill Road to Hawthorn Street; or of thousands of men, women and children hurrying to Petershill Park on Saturday afternoons to support the 'Peasies' as they sought victory in a Scottish Central League match or in a Scottish Junior Cup Tie. Springburn without people is like Punch without Judy. And that is why I was so dismayed at the desolation I witnessed when, three years or so ago, I returned to visit Springburn after an absence of some 20 years.

I was not born in Springburn, I was born in the country in Galloway, but I came to live in Springburn (up on the High Road near the Kinema) when I was 11 years old in 1948, and I lived in Springburn, with a short interruption when my mother moved house to Easterhouse, until moving to Cumbernauld in 1965 shortly after my second son was born. Springburn was my first taste of city life. Our tenement room and kitchen on the High Road was the first house I lived in which had running water; the first house which had a flush toilet (even if it was in the close); the first house which had fitted lighting—even it it was gas lamps; and the first house in which we had a fitted cooker rather than the hob and range of the coal fire. All of these new amenities and the hustle and bustle of thousands of people were a great wonder for a young boy from the country. And I loved all the activity. I remember the traffic jams as the great steam engines were brought out of the Hyde Park Works and taken on low-loaders down to the docks to be shipped to India or Africa. The great queue of trams—the No. 25, the No. 32, the No. 33—slowly following the crawling vehicles down Springburn Road, Parliamentary Road and Castle Street.

I remember the elections of 1951 and 1952 with huge public gatherings at Vulcan Street just across the road from the Cowlairs Road clock as the election candidates addressed the voters.

I remember the great excitement in Springburn when the 'Peasies' returned from Hampden with the Scottish Junior Cup, having 'mowed the meadow' from Irvine in 1950—or was it '51 or '52?—I am not sure of the year, but I can still remember the team—'Stewart, McNellis, McNab,' etc'.

All these are still vivid memories of a thriving, bustling, industrial community of about 30 000 people. A community with a heart and soul; a community with character and characters, despite the poor housing conditions in which most of us lived.

This book vividly captures these pictures and I think that many people will smile quietly and say as I have, 'I remember that' when they read the reminiscences of those interviewed in the book. I say 'smile quietly' because although the housing conditions were bad, and most households were dependent for survival on fairly low incomes, the camaraderie, the neighbourliness, the community feeling of one family for another was such that mostly warm memories remain.

It is these memories and these experiences, from Springburn, Bridgeton, Parkhead, the South Side, Govan and thousands of other smaller areas throughout Scotland, throughout the period since the Industrial Revolution which have moulded the Scottish character of warmth and concern for the community. Those who worship self and greed cannot understand these characteristics. They should read this book and perhaps it would help them to understand that their creed of greed will never be accepted by those who have experienced the warmth of real community.

Campbell Christie
February 1989

INTRODUCTION

Social history aims to understand the daily lives of the mass of the people in the past. To isolate a single strand, such as work, is artificial, but is convenient and draws attention to what may otherwise be taken for granted. Even today, with 3 million unemployed, the psychological importance of having paid employment is often underestimated. A job is not only the key to a person's standard of living, but in important ways is the basis of personal identity and self respect. Work is not merely an economic activity: it is a crucial human function, and, along with the family, is the most important way many people participate in society.

Springburn was built for work. It was a tiny village in the 1840s when the great factories of the industrial revolution attracted workers there from all over Britain. The lives of the individuals and the community which grew up were shaped by the work available there, and when that work ceased to be available, both individuals and community were damaged, both materially and psychologically. This book deals with paid work and mostly that of men, the traditional breadwinners. It is important to emphasise, however, that the local economy could not have functioned without the unpaid work of women, the majority of whom kept house and reared families. Those who did take up paid work, took it on in addition to these tasks. Also important and also excluded here are the voluntary activities of men and women who worked to create a better life for the community as a whole. Much of this was done through the churches, of which were were at least 17 in Springburn by the end of the First World War. Each had a great variety of organisations for men, women and children, providing important social, recreational and welfare as well as spiritual, services. However, these interviews concentrate on secular voluntary organisations directly related to paid work—friendly societies, co-operatives and trades unions.

This book deals with the experience of work in Springburn using the memories of local people as its main source. As part of a Community Programme training scheme, 120 local people were interviewed and the tapes transcribed. Most of the interviews cover the whole of a person's life history and the quotations about work comprise only a fraction of the whole. Originally, we hoped simply to present the relevant excerpts from the transcripts as a collection of primary sources. Using human memory as historical evidence has different problems from those associated with written evidence, and these made it necessary to provide a context and an explicit interpretation. With texts, hindsight is a problem, but usually only for the interpreter. With oral history it is part of the source as well—everyone views the past from the perspective of the present. With written sources it is possible to chart the change in attitudes; unless memories are recorded at different stages, it is much more difficult to evaluate changes in the attitudes of people who, for the most part, do not leave written records. In ten or twenty years, the same people may have completely different interpretations of the same events in their own lives, depending on how social changes affect them and their families. Thus, the interviews recorded here are as much about the 1980s as about the past: they represent how Springburn was remembered in the '80s, as much as how Springburn really was in the 1920s, '30s or '40s.

Another problem is the interview itself: subject and interviewer react to each other and adapt their answers and questions in response to what each says. Interviews are an evolving synthesis of themes. We cannot say we come to regard the past without any preconceptions —otherwise we would not have been interested in asking people questions. We were most struck by the features of the past which compare or contrast revealingly with the products of our own experience. Every oral history interview is essentially a compromise between what we want to ask and what the individual wishes to tell us. We hope we have achieved a balance between the two, that we have tested our preconceptions and that we have enabled the interviewee's own views to come through, so that readers can provide their own interpretations of the evidence if they are unhappy with ours.

The influence of contemporary pressures may help explain why one important theme is not treated in any detail in this work. At a time when such attitudes have less public acceptance and are associated with terrorism, it is perhaps understandable that most interviewees were reluctant to discuss the role of sectarianism in the workplace. As one informant, in refusing to discuss the subject, said: 'There was no sectarianism in St Rollox, but there were no Catholics either'. This, however is an exaggeration, applying at most to certain departments.

Most of those who were interviewed are no longer working. Most are retired, though many are people who were made redundant in their fifties and cannot, with rare exceptions, expect to find work again. Though retirement is not perhaps as alienating as unemployment, ceasing to work for whatever reason alters perceptions. It is from this viewpoint that most of the interviews are given—with people whose working lives are over, and who are looking back and evaluating. The interviews were carried out by young people who were on a Community Programme because they could not find work, and who had very little work experience. The older people grew up in a culture founded on heavy industry which for the space of a few generations appeared stable. The interviewers have grown up in a very different society, with far fewer skilled manual workers, more service workers, smaller workplaces, and all the other characteristics of a 'post-industrial' age. When the interviewees were young, they learned a great deal from their elders about how to work the labour market and about what to expect in their working lives. The memories of older people are no longer useful in this way, which is perhaps one of the reasons why conversations between these generations take place as part of a formal research project for a museum rather than spontaneously as part of normal social interaction. In a time of rapid change, one of the functions of the social history museum is to pool experiences and make them available to the community. What may not seem immediately useful to people preoccupied with finding a job may still give an important perspective and may have unpredictable uses in the future. Indeed, treating the experience of recent generations as history can help us see the process of coping with change more clearly, and so establish what should be retained from the past. This is especially true of Springburn where many older people feel that what they have to offer is a sense of the communal values which grew up in working class areas in response to industrial culture.

Oral history gives us an insight into how people feel and felt, their reactions to events outside their control, the degree to which they felt able to exercise choice and their judgements about consequences of the choices they made. No attempt has been made to retain all the accents and intonations of the spoken word. We hope, nonetheless, that some of the sensation of contact with real people comes through.

The photographs support the text but also have a story of their own to tell. In particular, they are very revealing about working clothes and conditions. Many aspects of people's working lives in the past were not photographed. So that the future generations would not face the difficulty of portraying the past with, at best, random surviving images, we undertook a photographic survey of a sample of modern workplaces. The selection reproduced here brings the story up to date, and provides a useful reminder of how different the experience of work is now, compared with the memories on which this book is based.

This is the earliest surviving photograph of housework in Springburn, taken about 1890. Every one of approximately 10,000 houses in Springburn used coal for heating and cooking. The smoke which blackened the walls of the tenements meant that cleaning windows, like washing clothes and other household tasks, was a far more laborious chore than at present. The unpaid work of housewives was a integral part of the local economy.

St Rollox blacksmiths in 1898.

ACKNOWLEDGEMENTS

Our greatest debt is to the many people who so generously shared their memories with us. Without their co-operation, this book would have been impossible and history would have been the poorer for the absence of the views of the people who lived through it.

Arthur Adams
James Aitcheson
Alice Amato
Joseph Amato
Margaret Burniston
Joseph Cairns
Campbell Christie
John Craig
William Dewar
Joseph Docherty
John Dowie
David Gould
Samuel Hoey
Fred Holmes
Bob Kenny
George Ingram
Dick Johnstone
Isobel Jordan
Alec MacGregor
William McGinley
Cathy McIlroy

Joseph McKay
Mr McLean
Douglas MacMillan
John Menzies
GD Morrison
Agnes Muirhead
Martha MacMillan
Cathy Page
Jean Parker
Ian Rankin
Catherine Richardson
Peter Russell
William Sancroft
Henry Stewart
Andrew Stuart
Andy Stuart
Jimmy Vaughan (RIP)
David Walters
Helen Woods (RIP)
John Wotherspoon

A special word of thanks is due to the supervisors of the MSC Community Programme, before Gerard Hutchison took over—Martin Roberts and Susan Jeffrey. We would also like to thank the young people who carried out the interviews, and Dallas Mechan, who worked with the project while on a training attachment from Leicester University's Museums Studies course.

Karen Cameron
Corrinne Carson
Carolyn Fitton
Gary Florence
John Fury
Alison Irwin
Sandra Kernahan
David Konnerth
Margaret Lamb

Jane Logue
Sarah-Jane McGinley
Peter McKenzie
Patricia Mullen
Larry O'Rourke
Liz Robertson
Pauline Sweeney
David Tamburrini
Colin Turner

We are grateful to Andy Stuart, Juliet Kinchin and Eileen Gordon for reading the text. Springburn Museum's managing agency for the Community Programme was the Glasgow Council for Voluntary Services, without whose administrative back-up we could not have maintained the project. In particular, without the unfailing support of Ian McCluskey, the publication of this book would not have taken place. The Manpower Services Commission not only funded the Community Programme but grant aided the printing costs. We are happy to acknowledge our gratitude for this support, which made both project and book possible.

Photographs

The photographs appear courtesy of the Mitchell Library, Strathclyde Regional Archives, The Springburn Museum and the following individuals: Robert Barr, Mrs Bennet, John Binnie, Eleanor Boyd, George Burns, Mary Christie, Mrs M Dey, George Dyce, Samuel Hoey, Angus Kean, Joseph MacKay, Martha MacMillan, John Gillespie, Marion Anderson, Douglas MacMillan, John & Annie Martin, Isa Nelson, John Scott, Andy Stuart, Betty Traynor and Betty Vaughan.

Photographs of modern Springburn by Susan Scott & Corrinne Carson.

BIBLIOGRAPHY

PRIMARY SOURCES

The Mitchell Library
General Strike 1926 papers
Springburn & St Rollox Advertiser

SCOTTISH RECORDS OFFICE
Rules of Hyde Park Locomotive Works Friendly Society
Rules of Keppochhill Friendly Society
Rules of Petershill Co-operative Society
Rules of Keppochhill Co-operative Society

SPRINGBURN MUSEUM
MacEwan, JF, St Rollox Works, A Brief Record (unpublished ms, 1986).
Martin, A, Memoirs (unpublished ms, 1981).
Morrison, GD, History of the Craigpark Electric Cable Company (unpublished ms, 1986).
Stuart, A, Metropolitan Vickers/Associated Electrical Engineering Industries 1953–1968 (unpublished ms, 1987).

The Springburn Sound Archive, which consists of 120 taped and transcribed interviews with people who lived or worked in the area.

SECONDARY SOURCES

Bremner, David, The Industries of Scotland, Their Rise, Progress and Present Condition (1869). Reprinted by David & Charles, 1969, with an introduction by John Butt and Ian L Donnachie.
Corporation of Glasgow & University of Glasgow, The Springburn Study, Urban Renewal in a Regional Context, no date.
Glasgow District Council Planning Department, The impact on the local community of the contraction of British Rail Engineering Ltd, Springburn (Committee Report, August 1985)
Lowe, JW, British Steam Locomotive Builders, (Goose & Sons, 1975.)
MacEwan, S, On the High C's, (John S Burns, Glasgow, 1973.)
Nicolson, M and **O'Neill M**, Glasgow: Locomotive Builder to the World, (Polygon Books, Third Eye Centre & Glasgow District Libraries Publication Board, 1987.)
Ralston, Andrew G, A History of St Rollox Church (Glasgow, 1984).
Thomas, J, The Springburn Story (David and Charles, 1964).

1

THE NINETEENTH CENTURY LEGACY

THE NINETEENTH CENTURY LEGACY

Most of Springburn's industries were founded in the second half of the nineteenth century. Right through their periods of growth, boom, slump, recovery and final decline in the late 1950s and '60s, they continued to be affected by their Victorian origins. These not only determined the physical environment, but also influenced working practices, training and recruitment procedures, attitudes to trades unions and innovations, and the social life surrounding the works. This chapter aims to give brief histories of the origins of the main industries in Springburn, showing both the dominance of the railway works, and the wide range of other industries which were attracted there by the location, and the opportunity to employ or provide services for a skilled workforce.

Moving to Springburn

In the years after 1840, Springburn industrialised rapidly and, apart from times of general slump, it was a place of high employment, so that people came from all over Britain looking for work. Many came from rural backgrounds, in the Scottish Highlands or Ireland. Springburn developed into a thriving community within two generations of its industrial boom, and it remained very much an immigrant town well into the twentieth century. In 1914, the Springburn wards had the highest proportion of Irish born in Glasgow. Depending on when they arrived, what the Springburn migrants found would have been radically different. For, in spite of an illusion of stability, Springburn has been changing rapidly and continually since its foundation.

Migration often involves leaving behind family and friends. However, once one member of a family established a base in a new place, other relatives benefitted. Campbell Christie, later General Secretary of the STUC, recalls his family's move to Springburn in the mid 1940s. 'My father worked ... in the granite quarry, and as a result of that he had a lot of trouble, stomach trouble, dust and whatever, and he died in 1944, and that left my mother with six surviving sons, all of whom were either under school age or at school. The two oldest were about to leave school, and my oldest brother came up to Glasgow to work, and he worked at Fairfield's as an apprentice draughtsman. My second oldest brother, he left school earlier, at the minimum age of fourteen, and he came to Springburn to work at Robertson's the joiner, as an apprentice joiner. That was in Keppochhill Road, just beside the Fire Station. We had relatives in Springburn—my mother's sister, and indeed her own mother had come up before the war to live in Glasgow ... the family originate from Kirkcudbrightshire/Wigtonshire ... so I suppose the first move up was my mother's sister. She lived in Drumbottie Road, and my mother's mother moved up with her, and my mother was looked after by an aunt in Kirkcudbrightshire, so, when my father died, and with no real prospect of employment other than in the quarry or on the land, it was perhaps fairly natural that ... my mother looked for the two older boys to come up to Glasgow, and they stayed with my aunt, and ... with the two of them here, my mother decided we should all move to Glasgow, and we moved up in 1947 or 1948 to Springburn Road.'

Though having greater economic opportunities, the city did not necessarily provide a better environment than the countryside. For Campbell Christie, the move to a room and kitchen was, on balance, an improvement:

'It was an advance because where we had lived, we had no gas or electricity, we had no running water, I mean ... in Kirkcudbrightshire we used to have to carry the water from a well to the house ... the only heating was fires and that was much the same. The only difference was that it was a cottage, and we had what would be a kitchen, living-room and bedroom, but upstairs there was an attic, and there were two rooms in the attic, so that gave us more space... So it wasn't a great sort of social disaster for us to come to Springburn.'

The railway industries

Working and living conditions in Kirkcudbrightshire in the 1940s are reminiscent of Springburn 100 years earlier, before the railways came. Then, there were two villages, one at Balgrayhill and another at Springburn Cross, inhabited by weavers, miners, quarry workers and agricultural labourers, domestic and farm servants. It would be wrong to romanticise these as peaceful hamlets—one contemporary source, relating to coal miners in Keppochhill refers to the 'humiliating effects of our appalling employ'. Nonetheless, they certainly must have experienced a shock in 1840–1 when some of the 15 000 railway navvies engaged in building the Edinburgh & Glasgow Railway line descended upon them. Because of their nomadic lives and harsh conditions, railway navvies were among the toughest and least 'respectable' of all workers (so hard was the work that it was said that it took a year to transform a agricultural labourer into a navvy). In December 1840, two navvies—Dennis Doolan and Patrick Redding—took exception to Doolan being sacked for insubordination and returned the following day and beat the offending foreman to death. They were hanged, not, as was customary, outside the court buildings in Glasgow, but a mile and half north of Bishopbriggs, as a grim warning to other navvies. They were brought by road in an open parcels-cart the six miles from Glasgow. By the time the procession, consisting of a body of 1st Dragoons, the City Marshal, Sheriff Allison, the culprits and a strong guard of cavalry and magistrates of the city, had reached the scaffold

B

at Crosshill, it had gathered a crowd of some 6000 people. The large escort was to pre-empt a rumoured plan by the navvies to rush the scaffold and free the prisoners. The hanging went ahead however, with Redding dying instantly ('the rope came down kindly enough,' as the executioner put it), but Doolan struggled violently for a long time. (Thomas, 1964, pp 35–40.)

Springburn's frontier character during its early days is confirmed by an early missionary to the Garngad and St Rollox areas, where Springburn merged into the city. He stated in 1854 that 'Intemperance, Sabbath Desecration, and other forms of wickedness prevail to a fearful extent in the district' (Dr Ralston, p. 3). It was at St Rollox that Springburn's first railway works were founded, a small concern, belonging to the Glasgow & Garnkirk Railway and built sometime between 1834–40.

The first major railway works, however, were built by the Edinburgh & Glasgow Railway Company, at the point where their line begins its steep descent to Queen Street Station. The works and the incline both took the name of the nearby Cowlairs estate. The new works soon superseded the E & G's Queen Margaret Works in Edinburgh. The first surviving description of it dates from 1868, when David Bremner wrote a series of articles for *The Scotsman* on the industries of Scotland, in which he included the Cowlairs Works:

'Excepting the cylinders, axle-boxes, and firebars, there is little or no cast iron used in the construction of a locomotive, while in the passenger-carriages and goods-waggons, only the axle-boxes and buffer-cylinders are made of that material. The foundry department at Cowlairs is on a considerable scale, and in it is made all the cast-iron work required for the company's locomotives, steamboats, carriages, and wagons, as well as a considerable quantity of castings for the permanent way. About fifty men are employed in the iron and brass foundries; but their operations do not call for special notice, all the work being of a simple kind. A large quantity of malleable iron is used, with the exception of the crank-axles, all the forgings are made at the works. The smithy is an immense place, containing upwards of sixty fires, and having among its fittings four steam hammers, which are kept going constantly. A great number of bolts and rivets are required, and these are turned out by the workmen at a rapid rate. The bolts are screwed at machines attended by boys, who are paid by piecework, and make excellent wages. One little fellow about twelve years of age is so expert that he makes ten or eleven shillings a week. In an adjoining place springs are made.

'The turning and fitting shops are abundantly supplied with all the appliances of a first-class engineering establishment, and there appears to be no end to the variety of operations that are carried on in them. Upwards of 5000 separate pieces of metal are used in the construction of a locomotive; and the making, adjusting, and uniting of these entails, as may be supposed, a vast expenditure of painstaking labour. The tires of the engine wheels are now for the most part made of steel by the ingenious process which dispenses with welding, and so lessens risk of breaking. None of the engine tires are made by the company, it being found most profitable and convenient to obtain these, as well as the crank-axles, from firms who devote special attention to their production.

'In the boiler-shop, about 120 men and boys are employed. The boilers, with the exception of the inner shell of the fire-box, are made of the best iron, in plates half an inch thick. In consequence of the intense heat of the furnace, the firebox is made of copper of the same thickness as the iron. The boiler plates, after being shaped, punched, and bent, are riveted together by a machine which is capable of doing as much work in two hours as half a dozen men could accomplish in a day, and in a much superior style. Two men and a boy are required to work the machine.

'When the parts of an engine are ready to be put together, they are taken to the erecting-shop, in which a special class of workmen called "erecters" are employed. There the engine is completed, and steam got up, and thence, radiant in paint and polished brass, it goes forth a thing of beauty and of strength, ready to do good service alike to prince and to peasant.

'The carriage building department comes next under notice. There, huge logs of timber are converted into carriages, waggons, and vans, by the hands of upwards of 400 workmen, aided by a large assortment of beautiful machines. The logs are conveyed by rail to the saw-mill, where they are cut by vertical and circular steam-saws into planks of the required dimensions. The planks are piled in a drying shed, and, after remaining there a certain time, are taken to the cutting-out shop, where they are planed, moulded, morticed, tenoned, and bored by machine. Every piece is fashioned according to a standard pattern, and little skill is required on the part of the workmen. They have to make scarcely a single measurement or calculation, but simply to mark the wood according to the patterns and place it in the machines.

'When the wood leaves the cutting-shop it is returned to the dry-shed, where it remains until required by the carriage builders. The latter occupy a vast range of workshops, in which carriages in all stages of completion may be seen. The frames of the carriages are of oak, and the planking of fir; but in the first class carriages a good deal of teak is used. There is in all classes of carriages a considerable quantity of iron work, which is brought from the smithy in a finished state. The carriage and waggon builders have everything prepared to hand, and they have simply to put the materials together. They are paid according to piece-work, and generally two or four work together and contract to build a carriage or waggon for certain sum. The building of goods and cattle waggons is a coarser kind of work; but for these the wood is prepared in the same way as for passenger carriages. The working power is equal to producing fifty waggons and six passenger-carriages a month. In the finishing department, women are employed in making the trimmings of first class carriages. The painting-shop is on a scale of vastness commensurate with the other parts of the establishment. In it the carriages are painted and varnished, and when they leave it are ready for use on the line.

So far as practicable, piece-work is the rule at Cowlairs, and is attended with the most satisfactory results to employers and employees. When piece-work was first proposed, some of the men demurred, until they discovered that they could thereby increase their wages by a few shillings a week; and, in certain cases, men are making thirty per cent more money than they received for the same number of hours when paid according to time. Fifty-eight hours a week is the working time throughout the establishment, and the average rate of wages is as follows:—Locomotive department—moulders, turners, and boiler-makers, 27s a week; smiths, fitters, and erectors, 26s; machine attendants, 20s; boiler-makers' assistants, 18s; boys, from 4s to 10s. Carriage building department—carriage builders and joiners, 24s to 26s a week; painters, 24s; machine attendants, 15s.'

It is not difficult to read between the lines of Bremner's enthusiasm and to discern what conditions in Cowlairs were like, though they were probably well up to standard compared to other works at the time. Joseph McKay began working in the Cowlairs brass finishing shop in 1911. In spite of the extent of mechanisation described by Bremner, Mr McKay recalls the high level of skill required:

'In those days when you were a boy, you did all your turning with your hands. You held the tool in your hands. Aye, you scraped threads with them, with a comb, and you scraped the thread and everything with it. I mean folk wouldn't believe the things we had to do. It was screwed up to eight threads to the inch by hand, that was inch Whitworths, that was the heaviest thread you could do... You had different shapes of tools and another thing you did, you would drop it into this stove, when your tools were needing drawn out a bit, you know, it had been ground too far back. And we forged our own tools, ground them, and tempered them, all ready for work again... When I went in there at first, there was no electricity. No electricity, it was round lamps, incandescent lights that were on the roof. What you had at your bench was the same as what you had at the houses, you know, you had long thin gas pipes, and a fishtail burner ... that's what you worked with.'

Not all the workers who came to Springburn in the early days were of rural origins. Many were already city dwellers with urban trades. The first 350 employees of the Caledonian Railway's new St Rollox Works were already working for the company in their overcrowded Greenock works. This large concern incorporated the old Glasgow & Garnkirk Works, which became the boiler shop. The CR agreed to issue the men with passes to seek out accommodation when the company moved from Greenock to Springburn in 1856. The company also 'flitted' the men, their families and their possessions to St Rollox, but did not pay for moving their effects from St Rollox to their new homes. (McEwan, 1986, pp 4–5.)

St Rollox expanded steadily over the next 30 years. In 1868, a new wagon shop and paint shop were built, and an engine shed in 1879. There was often a time lag between the increase in the workload and the erection of buildings, so that work had to be carried on in the open air. Working without waterproofs in all weathers was one of the most unpleasant, not to say unhealthy, features of work at this period. There was always some work which had to be done outside, as in the Cowlairs wagon yard, which was known as Siberia. Not that the interiors were much better, as they were unheated until after 1945. By the time St Rollox was taken over by the London Midland & Scottish Railway, gas and later, electric light had been installed and overhead belting and line shafting removed. By the 1930s, the LMS had introduced efficiencies into the way the work was organised, using the 'belt system' for repairs of locomotives and the apparently novel idea of working to a time schedule. (McEwan, 1986, p. 6.)

In 1895, St Rollox covered 23 acres with buildings accounting for about 12 of these. In 1902, 3130 men worked there. After the 'Grouping' of the private railway companies in 1923, St Rollox became part of the LMS, who soon afterwards reduced it to a repair depot. The transfer of the manufacture of steam engines to the south was a keenly felt loss among workers. The early days after amalgamation are remembered by Arthur Adam: 'I can remember going down to the Caley, and going in through the main gate, through where the forging was done, through the smiddy, in to the main machine shop, which in those days was a mass of belt drives. A main big motor for longitudinal shafts at the top of the machine shop. Then you had other drives coming off that, driving all the machines. Just a mass of belts. And they employed a belt man in the shop for repairing them, all these belts in the machine shop. And I went through the machine shop into the erecting shop. And I got my eyes opened in there ... every locomotive was actually different from the one next to it. Lots of variations in classes and so on.'

Cowlairs became part of the London and North Eastern Railway in 1923 and was also reduced to a repair shop. In 1948, nationalisation brought both the works into British Rail. The change to diesel and the

Beeching cuts of the 1960s led to a nationwide reduction in the number
of railway works. The Cowlairs works were closed in 1968 and its
workers transferred to St Rollox, which was completely modernised.
Renamed the Glasgow Works, it was hived off to a separate company
—British Rail Engineering Ltd—in 1971. Further reduction in capacity
and centralisation in the south led in 1986 to the BREL works being
reduced to a British Rail Maintenance Ltd depot, with the loss of 1600
jobs.

John Menzies looks back on a working life spent entirely in St
Rollox, beginning in 1942:

'St Rollox suffered, and I suppose Cowlairs would too, from the
railway grouping. We've been considering the demise of Springburn,
but this didn't start with the war, or Dr Beeching or anybody like that,
but long before. It would be I suppose in 1923, when the railways were
grouped, and St Rollox and Cowlairs became outstations, really, of the
Crewe–Derby axis on one side and Doncaster on the other, that they
only got what was handed down to them from these works.

'I remember some of the men in St Rollox were still very sore about
the fact that some machinery had been taken from St Rollox to Crewe.
I understand that a massive slotting machine, which was used for
slotting frames—it could do about a dozen frames at the one time—and
this had been in St Rollox in Caledonian times, and was removed to
Crewe, where, I understand, I don't know but I understand, it was used
for the manufacture of the frames for the Stanier *Duchesses* and the
later British Railways express locomotives.

'And of course all work was withdrawn from St Rollox. Some of
it did linger on for a bit, during the 1920s, but I believe the last new
engine was built in St Rollox in 1928 or 1929. They continued building
some of the 60 Class, which was designed by Mr Pickersgill, who was
the Superintendent before the grouping, and they also were given some
Midland designed 0-6-0 engines—the 4Fs. After that, the place just
became a repair shop, and they introduced—it had been introduced
before I got there—a 'Belt System', as they called it for the repair of
locomotives. The locomotive was supposed to stay in the works for
about six days, and I remember they had a big diagram up in the
Erecting Shop with six pictures of a Black 5, showing it from just the
bare frame to ready to go out the door—what was supposed to be done
each day. I can't remember how closely they stuck to these times. Some
of it would be quite impossible to stick to; if an engine came in damaged
for example, it would require extra work done on it.

'They had to change in St Rollox, of course, from the Caledonian
system, which was rather an odd system really, in that every locomotive had its own boiler. It came in with the boiler and the boiler was
repaired and the engine was repaired and it all went out together,

whereas the LMS system had spare boilers, and if a locomotive came in with a boiler which needed a lot of work, it was just sent off to the boiler shop and there was another one brought in, which seems a sensible engineering thing to do.

'The standard of work may have dropped when it ceased to be a new building works, because I'm sure the morale of the workforce did fall. It must have done. Thinking back and recalling some of the older hands talking, I'm sure they were upset at having lost this facility. Everybody says, of course, it was much better in the old days, but even making allowances for that, there was, I'm sure, a sense of pride in these Caledonian engines which they built, which was totally missing by the time they came to just repair Black 5s, with no criticism of the Black 5s, but it was built somewhere else, and it was only being maintained at St Rollox. It didn't really belong to St Rollox.'

Private locomotive builders

As well as the railway works run by companies which also owned traffic departments, there were two other works, owned by private builders who sold engines to railway companies at home and abroad. Both of these works were founded by Walter Montgomerie Neilson (1819–1889). He was a son of James Beaumont Neilson, inventor of the hot blast method of smelting iron, which played a key role in the industrial revolution in Scotland. He began making locomotives in Hyde Park Street, Finnieston, with various partners, and adjacent to the family business. In 1862, he opened a new works in Springburn, naming it after the street in which he had started up. The move gave him more space than the cramped Clydeside site. His main customers at this time were British railway companies and the new location had direct access to the whole rail network through the Edinburgh & Glasgow line. Neilson's first manager, Henry Dubs, left in 1863 to set up his own works, the Glasgow Locomotive Company, in Queen's Park on the south side of the city. Dubs' successor at Hyde Park was James Reid who bought out Neilson in 1872. This deal was concluded amid great acrimony which led to a court case, which Neilson lost. He spent most of the next decade abroad, but in 1884 he returned to Glasgow to set up a new locomotive works. One can readily imagine a certain malice, or at least righteousness, in his choice of site—directly opposite his old works. He called it the Clyde Locomotive Works. It was unable to drum up business however and in its first four years built only 23 engines. Neilson therefore sold out, to Sharp Stewart of Manchester. The lease on their Atlas Works in Manchester was running out and they were attracted by the lower rates and wages in Glasgow, by the presence of a skilled workforce and a completely new, modern plant.

The Hyde Park works were described in the July 1895 edition of *The Engineer*:

'Since the removal to Springburn the business has steadily grown. In 1965 about 1000 men were employed, and the output was 82 engines; the present establishment when fully equipped employs over 2500, turns out more than 200 main line engines a year; it is thus the largest of the kind in Great Britain.

'The new offices built in 1887, comprising the commercial and drawing departments, are the latest addition to the works, and are a model of convenience. The other various departments are arranged with a view to the regular sequence of work being followed throughout. The pattern shop leads to the brass and iron foundries and coppersmiths' shop, the template shop, and the boiler and tender shops, parallel to which are the smithy and the forge. The boiler shop contains a hydraulic flanging press for locomotive plates, special machines for drilling boilers together and apart, hydraulic riveter, &c. In another large block of buildings, opposite to the boiler shop and smith, and parallel to one another, are the grinding, finishing, turning, machine, wheel and frame and boiler-mounting shops, finishing with the erecting shop, the focus of the work from all the other departments. A spacious steaming shed serves to relieve the erecting shop after the engines have been put together, and enables work to be stored if there is any delay between completion and shipment. The packing and painting shops complete the works. The locomotives made here are of all classes, and examples of them are to be found on almost all railways. The total output to the present time amounts to nearly 5000 engines, which, if placed end to end, would extend over thirty miles.'

In 1903, the Hyde Park, Atlas, and Queen's Park works were amalgamated to form the North British Locomotive company, the largest firm of its kind in Europe. This employed 8000 workers and had the capacity to build 600 engines a year. The company came more and more to rely on export orders and its engines had to be hauled through the streets to the dockside at Finnieston, close to where the old Neilson works were. The majestic sight of the engines being hauled through the streets is one that, for most Springburn people, defines the positive aspects of the industrial past that has now disappeared. It embodied an unrivalled level of craft and skill, recognised in the worldwide demand for its products.

However, the NBL's orders never reached its capacity at amalgamation and, apart from booms associated with the two World Wars, it was in decline from 1905 onwards. The wars created an illusion of a strong market, which reinforced a reluctance to innovate. The delay in changing to diesel, the breakup of the British Empire, the nationalisation of the Argentine railways and protectionism amongst developing and Commonwealth countries all contributed to the decline. The delay in responding to the collapse of the international market for steam engines was also due to its being interpreted as a temporary slump, such as had happened periodically in the 19th century. During the slack periods, it was the Atlas works which suffered, being closed down in 1923, and the core of skilled workers maintained in the other two works. The company reached its lowest ebb in the depression of the 1930s, making only 16 engines in 1933. Nonetheless, even in 1960, two years before its final closure, NBL employed 5000 men, most of them in well-paid skilled jobs.

The works run by private locomotive companies had a different atmosphere from those run by companies which had traffic departments as well. Though on a large scale, the former retained something of the family firm. In NBL's works, a strong paternalistic welfare tradition in the management was matched by a great loyalty to the company amongst workers. On the other hand, workers in the LMS and LNER works were better paid and were more unionised. They also had excursions, privilege tickets (usually half the single fare) and one free family ticket for the annual holidays.

Office work

All four railway works had large office staffs. Catherine Richardson recalls her first years as an office girl in Cowlairs:

'Well, from the beginning I was the office girl, but (had) different jobs when I got older a bit. The first day I had to be in at half past eight, but the time of the office was nine till five. The office boy and I, we had to open all the letters and then we'd to divide them out into the departments that they belonged to, and if it was the accountant's private letters we took them into his room and changed his calendar and then take the different departments' letters up to them—Wages and the Engine Department. We delivered them before nine o'clock, so everything was ready when people came in at nine o'clock. We opened and registered the letters in a book ... then the number we registered them, when they wanted any letter, they came back and told us this register number and went up in the filing, looked and gave them out the copies so they could get it. They don't do that now exactly, but that's the way we did it. And after that we used to go around the departments to see if anybody wanted any tickets, then I used to go up the road—I don't know whether it was official or unofficial—for cakes for their morning tea. Because we didn't have things they have nowadays, proper—we just had a big gas ring and a kettle and you made your own tea... Eventually I was on the book-keeping machine. It was a big machine, like that it was made by Elliot Fisher and it did, you know, we kept the records of the work that came in. They came in on one side, you know, the issue of the jobs and the work, they were manufactured by a move order, what we called a move order in the works ... the machine subtracted it all and we put the heading of whatever it was, if it was a bolt or something like that, and a certain size.'

George Ingram began working for NBL as a storeboy:

'As a storeboy my duties were to look after the drawings that were used for the manufacture of locomotives and at the time they were also manufacturing a small tank, we used to call it a whippet tank. I don't know if that was the proper name for it ... but in the store we looked after the drawings and we were taught at this time, it was a cardinal offence if you folded the drawings in any way. Drawings must be rolled out and for storage space you needed a large area because the drawing had to be opened out and spread flat and the utmost care had to be used looking after these drawings.'

At a more senior level, James Aitcheson worked as an accountant in St Rollox, where his father had been a foreman:

'One interesting thing about the works was the machine shop. I had to know what each machine was able to produce and what the men did produce on it. I went into the New Work's section in the accountant's in 1929, and any new machines... You had to have some understanding of what they did, and what the new machine was capable of, because you used to try and save half a man. You couldn't halve a man, so you had to spread that work, and that man's full-time job went on to other machines. Naturally you had to know what the other engines were capable of, and whether they were occupied the full eight hours, or only six hours. You had to spread that man's work over three machines to justify the existence of the new machine... You had to justify production. It was a bit like time and motion. For instance, the carriage shop would put the underframes onto movement every half an hour, and there were certain jobs that had to be done in that half hour before that underframe moved up to the coachbuilding, and that was run away in another shop. For instance, the boiler shop took the boilers off, that went to the boiler shop, whereas the wheels and motion and that remained in what they called the erection shop, that then was timed to have that boiler ready by the time the underframe was ready—the workshop foremen organised all this.

'"Piece-work", as we were taught, "was a consideration granted by an employer to an employee to stimulate production/output." That was in the class of accountancy at night school. You had a piece-work price for most of the jobs in St Rollox, and I remember the men used to go down to see the foremen for the next job, and if their one job had been an extra good price, they'd maybe get a job at a cheaper price to balance out their piece-work at the end of the week. The shops and the jobs were independent. If you were a fitter, you had your piece-work prices for your particular job. If you were a cabinet maker, certain jobs carried their own piece-work price—it depended on the trade. Shops negotiated their prices because one squad might not do the same job again. But when you came to the machine shop, for instance, the jobs were priced according to the capability of the machine. Because you'd one machine doing piston-rings, and it was working quicker than the other, the piece-work price was adjusted accordingly. At that time the foreman would calculate the speed of the machine. Whereas later on they got what were called piece-work price setters. That was later on. They were all tradesmen, they knew the job. Accountants had nothing to do with the actual setting of the prices. But we knew the prices, and we were able to spot check. But that was the wages section. I wasn't in the wages section, so I couldn't say about the frequency of the checks. I was in New Works—new machinery and alterations, improvements in locomotives and carriages. I'd all the rolling stock to take into account too. A dozen people in my section. In the wages section there was a routine, you were tied to Friday pay, therefore they had to be busy right away on Monday, because it had to be ready by the Wednesday. You had to advise the bank on the money required. We got the time sheets from the timekeeper—we got all the slips from the workshops themselves, up into the office on the Monday morning, and those wage slips went through the foremen in each different office. There were a lot of workshop offices, one for the carriage shop, one for the paint shop, etc etc.'

Along with the men who worked in the railway factories, many traffic department workers—drivers, firemen, guards, signalmen—lived in Springburn. Springburn had four railway stations: Springburn, Barnhill, Cowlairs and St Rollox, of which only the first two survive, as do the Eastfield Running Sheds.

Other industries

The factors which made Springburn attractive to the railway works also appealed to other industries. A Glasgow directory of 1888 described the choice of site by Braby's for their Eclipse Works which they established in Petershill Road about 1880, moving there from Garngad Road: 'The position is in the very heart of the Scottish coal and iron fields, and thus economy is effected in the purchase of the leading requisites of the industry. For the purposes of transport and shipment also the works are admirably placed. They possess sidings from the North British, City of Glasgow Union, Caledonian and Glasgow and South Western Railways: and the Clyde, too, close at hand, affords means of direct shipment to almost any and all parts of the world.' Even with the high level of skill available in Springburn, Braby's imported many of its specialised workers from the south, so that 145, 151 and 163

Petershill Road were known as the 'English' tenements. It manufactured galvanised and corrugated iron, and a wide range of products made from these materials. 'The process known as galvanising, it may be well to remark, is of comparatively recent introduction, and consists in coating the iron to be treated with zinc by immersion, the zinc being dissolved in a tank with a flux of muriate of ammonia. The process presents a very inexpensive and effective means of protecting the metal from oxidation, and is applicable to any class of exposed ironwork.' In the annealing department sheets of metal 'are "annealed" or tempered, in such a way as to reduce their brittleness: and so effective is the process that after having undergone it the sheets can be worked almost as easily as copper. The annealing furnace ... will anneal from 70 to 80 tons of iron plates per week. The corrugating shop ... has an ample complement of steam-power rolls and presses for imparting the necessary corrugations to roofing and other building iron in sheets. Adjoining the corrugating shop are the joiners' and packing-case makers' department, and across the spacious yard is the drawing loft, where drawings of roofing in progress of production are made in full size on the floor, and templates taken there for the guidance of the workmen. Then there are blacksmiths shops, a separate department for the making of iron buckets and hollow ware, and busy tinsmiths shops, all in constant activity and full operation: and in each of these departments have numerous labour-saving mechanical appliances to assist them in their work.' There were 350 men employed there, and if we can judge from later accounts of working conditions, recorded at a time when health and safety legislation was much tougher, it had the worst working environment in Springburn.

During the Second World War, Alice Amato worked in both Braby's and in the St Rollox Works and was in a good position to compare them:

'We worked in tents there (St Rollox), the welders, you know, on your own... Aye canvas, you know square canvas. You were all in a row, but it was different in Braby's, really it was better because you werenae giving sore eyes to anybody, whereas in Braby's anybody passing would get flashes... It was completely different work from Braby's you know... Though in the welding you were quite busy, in the other parts of the work that you could walk through, you know you could go for a walk in the Caley, which you couldnae do in there. Men were sitting enjoying themselves instead of getting stuck in. So I says to Joe when I met him, "What a difference between the Caley and Braby's... They don't work half as hard as you do." It was a holiday tour, going to the Caley, you know. Only we had longer hours, we had to do a twelve hour shift.'

In sharp contrast with the harsh conditions in Braby's were those in the Craigpark Cable Works, which moved to Springburn from Dennistoun in 1903. Expanding from being golf-ball makers to include a wide range of electric cables, it had the reputation of having the best working conditions and staff-employee relations in the area, at least in the post-war period. Margaret Burniston recalls:

'I started in the rubber shop and I worked at a forcing machine as they called it—it was a drum of wire and I turned it, and it went through a machine similar to a mincer ... (and) went through a tank of water to cool and then it was packed in big round pans. (The atmosphere) was good, nice, not very with it. Now during the war we got all our modern things, canteens, there was no canteens or anything like that in a work then and when you got your holidays at Christmas and in the Fair you didn't get paid. You got ten days at Christmas, ten days holidays at the Fair, and you weren't paid for these holidays.'

G. Morrison was chief chemist at Craigpark. As specifications about the quality of materials used became more stringent, his job became more sophisticated, and took on a function akin to quality control. His job involved 'testing of all incoming materials. It was particularly interesting work because there was such a colossal range of material. We'd many, all the various chemicals and rubber components, plastic components, ingredients went into them, the various metals, the fabrics, quite a lot of fabrics went into the cables in those days, varnished cambrics and various proof cottons and so on, that these have been largely superseded by plastics and as I say there were various metals, conductors, lead for the sheafing, steel wires, steel tape for arming the cables... But also in addition to all that, increasingly we sort of stuck our noses into processing. As the processes became more complicated they had to get away from the old idea of a fellow picking up a piece of rubber and biting it—he's a foreman, he knew whether this was right or wrong. Everything had to be to specification... In addition to checking all the incoming materials we were very much involved in all the processing, the mixing of the rubber compounds and checking the various processes, vulcanising for instance ... and what we called the paper cable side. In those days the power cables were all insulated by being wrapped in a very high quality paper. After the conductors were wrapped with paper we then called that a core and these cores were wrapped round onto big steel trays, enormous things about twelve feet across and these were lowered into a tank set way into the floor. You had maybe three or four of these great trays down and a lid was put on that and the air was pumped out. We achieved a high degree of vacuum. From time to time we would check for moisture content of the stuff that the vacuum pumps were pumping out ... once it was down to a certain level a hot mixture of oil and rosin was run in and stuck right into the dried and evacuated paper, and after these cores were thoroughly impregnated you might have one of them but commonly several of them were stranded together, laid up we called it. They were then as quickly as possible sheathed with lead—this was to keep the moisture out—and the lead was coated with bitumen because in case of the cables, folks expected a life of at least 25 years—you might think lead would last forever: it doesn't, and it was very important to coat the lead on the outside with either petroleum jelly or bitumen to keep the air out of it. After that it would be lapped with bitumenised hessian. They called this a bedding, that is, it was a bedding for the steel wires or the steel tape which we then would put on to armour the cable: loads of bitumen poured onto it and some whitewash to take away the tackiness. It was found in a drum and then went out the door.'

Craigpark had taken over a building which already had a chequered history. It had been built as a pottery but had seen two owners and had lain empty for a number of years in between. Both the Springburn Pottery and the Campbellfield Pottery had gone out of business as a result of foreign competition. When it became apparent by the mid 1950s that thorough modernisation was required, the directors decided that the building was unsuitable. Rebuilding was considered but rejected due to the level of capacity in the industry and the state of the market. Craigpark therefore closed down in July 1955. The site was bought by William Teacher & Sons Ltd who built a whisky bottling plant there in 1961, retaining only the Craigpark office block, which was a recent addition (1932). When it opened it was the most technologically advanced plant of its kind in Scotland, but in 1988 it was closed as part of the 'rationalisation' subsequent to Teacher's being taken over by DCL. Over 200 jobs were lost, with the result that the DHSS is now the largest single employer in the area.

Manufacturing industry provided the economic base for the community, but it was not the only source of work. The services people required provided a whole range of jobs: shopkeepers, teachers, doctors, chimney sweeps, ministers, building workers, tailors, street sweepers, insurance men and many more. The largest single employer apart from the metal industries was the Cowlairs Co-operative Society. Founded by employees of the North British Railway, it was designed to combat overcharging by local shopkeepers. Beginning with one shop in 1881, by the First World War it was the largest retail organisation in the north of the city. Its nearest rival in scale was Hoey's, 'Glasgow's Largest Cash Store', but there were also a myriad of small shops as well as tea rooms, bakeries, dairies, newsagents, butchers and so on. These were often family owned, or else were branches of famous city-wide chains such as Bayne and Duckett or the City Bakeries. Springburn was a mecca for shoppers for miles around.

The other significant employers were Stobhill Hospital (1904) and Foresthall Hospital, formerly the Poor House. Isa Nelson worked in both, in Stobhill for seven and a half years from the early fifties, and in Foresthall for 22 years from 1962:

'It was the holiday time and they were taking on temporary staff. So I went up, to see if I could get a job as a domestic, because the hours would suit me. It was half past seven to half past four. So I worked as a domestic. I got the job, and a big lecture telling me that if anything happened—your children werenae well and all that—you had to have somebody look after them. Fortunately at that particular time my mother was alive so my mother was able to look after them. And I quite enjoyed the job, thoroughly enjoyed it—heavy hard work. You used old fashioned jocks to polish the floor. Big high dusting brushes—you name it—and I could swing a jock! I really became quite interested in nursing. I worked with this sister—as a domestic in those days you helped in the ward, you worked according to what the sister of the ward felt. It wasnae like nowadays. Your boss was the sister of the ward and if she said make the beds you made the beds. But then I took a heart attack, twenty-five or twenty-seven years ago, and they told me that domestic work was too heavy. So one year later, I went to Foresthall and took my training as a enrolled nurse. I had to sit an entrance exam. If you didnae have your Highers, which they didnae have at my time, you had to sit an entrance exam. I went out to go for my shopping, ended up I went in to see if they were needing anyone, thinking in terms of a job as an auxiliary, and they spoke me into taking my training. I went and sat the exam and I knew that day I had passed and I was taken on as a pupil nurse. I worked there for twenty-two years and I thoroughly enjoyed it, I really did. As a domestic I done the cleaning in the ward. Quite often I done the cleaning and I done all the diets. I was in a medical ward and they done various diets—people with ulcers got a drink of fluid every hour, reduction diets, diabetic diets. They all came from the kitchen but I served them, so I had to know what I was doing. So part of my domestic training done me good when I went to work in Foresthall. You see they were short of nurses and the domestic fitted in and helped. I was young, nosey, asked questions.

'It was an entirely different world in Foresthall, because you were in direct contact with the patient. You were working with the patient and enrolled nurses. You started at half past seven. Obviously the enrolled nurse's duty was—she took the writing report. The other girls all worked on a sort of basis that you didnae go in dead on half past seven, you went in a wee bit before, took the report and started right away to get the patients up. When I say get the patients up, that was anybody who could manage their breakfast better sitting. There was this fight against keeping them in bed, but it had to depend if the patient was able to sit and take their breakfast, sitting on a chair and a wee table in front of them. The patient up, you put them on a commode, dressed them, put them beside their bed, moved on. And before the back of eight you had 24 patients up. A good morning would be if you had an enrolled nurse and two auxiliaries. Then you stripped the beds, maybe you had a few patients in bed, so the enrolled nurse and an auxiliary went and she done the bed patients, and the other nurse would strip the beds ready for getting the beds made. Now you had your beds and the ward tidy before half past nine. Then the enrolled nurse went for her breakfast first. Twenty minutes, you came back, done your medicines and the other two lassies went for their breakfast. And in between you're giving them bedpans or toilet roll, whatever was needed. And you were all go right up until dinner time, and for half past eleven you tried to have everything done—medicine, place all tidied, dusted, the lot—and ready to serve out your dinners at a quarter to twelve. If you had a good team you could have your dinners out and the three of us that had been on in the morning went for their half hour dinner break. Came back and washed their faces, tidying them up, and if there was a sitting room, which quite a lot of the wards did have, you'd have them in the sitting room in the morning and you'd bring them in to their bedside in the afternoon. But if it was a good ward where you didnae have anybody in bed, you kept them in the sitting room for the afternoon and then brought them in just after three. And afore you left at half past four, you had the report and everything to write, to tell who was ever coming in at your back what was happening. Plus you were bathing most days. Actually if you kept yourself well enough in advance you could sneak an odd smoke or a cup of tea, but if you were caught at it, God help you!'

Decline

The traditional industries were dependent on the railways being the main carrier of passengers and freight and on fragile export markets. They were thus devastated by the challenge of road transport and the collapse of the international market for steam engines. In the past, there had been regular layoffs and periods of short-time working during slumps. There was always, however, the expectation of working once things 'picked up'. By the middle 1950s, the slump had become terminal decline: 'Between 1954 and 1966 twenty-seven other manufacturing establishments in the Springburn Employment Exchange Area closed down and F Braby & Co., although continuing in other production, closed their rolling mill and structural steel department.' (Corporation of Glasgow/University of Glasgow, paragraph 4.5.) The result of this is that unemployment now stands at 27%. The breakup of the community and increase in material prosperity means that unemployment today is a much more solitary experience than in the 1930s. In addition, the scale of Springburn's workplaces created a dependence on a few large employers, so that people are ill-placed to respond to advice to set up their own businesses.

These changes have seriously affected the quality of life in the area. The loss of business, and the movement of people away, due to unemployment and redevelopment, forced many of Springburn's once famous shops to close. A similar fate overtook Springburn's five cinemas, many of the schools and churches and most of the small grocery shops. Civic amenities such as its public halls, its magnificent Winter Gardens and its swimming baths have been shut down as being too expensive to maintain. At its peak, around 1900, 30 000 people lived in central Springburn. The number today is less than 8000, but is roughly the same if one includes the surrounding estates in Sighthill, Red Road, Balornock and Barmulloch.

Before the decline, the vast majority of people lived there to be near their workplaces. Today, the vast majority of those who have jobs travel outside the area to work, reflecting in miniature, worldwide changes in the economy and especially in transport. Springburn was a creation of steam railways. The line which passed through it on the way from Edinburgh to Glasgow brought it closer to Scotland's industrial capital and gave it access to the entire British rail network. This was a precondition for the establishment of four locomotive works in the area, manufacturing steam engines first for the home and then for overseas markets. The development of road transport however destroyed the market for steam, and made commuting possible. This change is represented most powerfully by the expressway which passes through where the old centre of Springburn used to be. However, despite the unconscionable harm it has done, it is the expressway which now offers Springburn its best hope for revival. It means the motorway is only three minutes away, connecting Springburn to the rest of Britain in the way the railways did in the past.

C

The opening of the Glasgow and Garnkirk Railway in 1831. The line passed through the southern end of Springburn, where the company built a small works. This was later absorbed into the St Rollox Works. The early steam engine has no cab for the driver and fireman, who would have had to work in all weathers.

Steam hammer in Cowlairs Forge in 1914. The man third from the right was deaf and dumb. Co-ordination between the workers was essential for safe and efficient working. The noise of the hammers however would have meant that experience and signals were more important than speech.

Cowlairs boiler shop, 1921. The boy in the centre of the photograph is a rivet heater or 'hodder on'.

Cowlairs engine erecters, 1897. In the foreground right is a locomotive spring, and another can be seen on the engine behind.

Cowlairs erecting shop about 1900.

Cowlairs carriage builders, 1921. Long after they had ceased to build locomotives, Cowlairs and St Rollox built carriages and wagons. This involved a wide range of woodworking skills.

Cowlairs coachpainters c 1900.

Brass Finishing Shop in Cowlairs in 1916. Mr Joseph MacKay is third from the right at the back, with his arms folded.

Mr MacKay (far right) on his retirement in 1961, after fifty years in Cowlairs. Very few workers today can expect to spend their entire working lives with one company.

'A first class locomotive may indeed be said to be the greatest achievement of the mechanical engineer'. (David Bremner, 1869, p99).

Aerial view of St Rollox about 1955.

The end of an era—the last steam repair in the St Rollox Works.

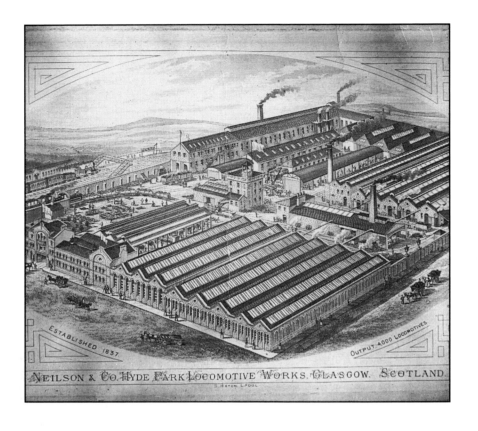

The Hyde Park Works in Ayr Street, about 1890.

The 25,000th locomotive built by the North British Locomotive Company. The drawing office staff sit proudly in front of this wartime austerity engine.

An engine decorated for an excursion by Eastfield (North British Railway) workers to Broughty Ferry on 10 September 1910.

Office staff in newly modernised offices in St Rollox about 1968.

Harry Howard, driver at Eastfield Shed on the day of his retiral 26.2.1965. The engine is number 45371 (ex-LMS 5,000). 'A keen eye, a steady hand, and a clear judgement are essential qualities in a driver, and to these must be added the power of close application to duty.' (David Bremner, 1869, p103).

Part of the Corrugating and Curving department of Braby's Eclipse Works in Petershill Road.

Members of the stranders section of the Craigpark Electric Cable Company in the late 1940s.

The Co-op had quickly moved from retailing to processing and manufacturing. This is the Cowlairs Co-operative Dairy in Angus Street about 1950. Betty McKinley (left) and Jean Minorgan are moving bottles from the machine into crates.

Hoey's shop about 1914

Christie's Grocer's shop, 22 Keppochhill Road. The decline of the community and competition from supermarkets led to its closure in 1976.

Isa Nelson at Stobhill Hospital, in the mid 1950s.

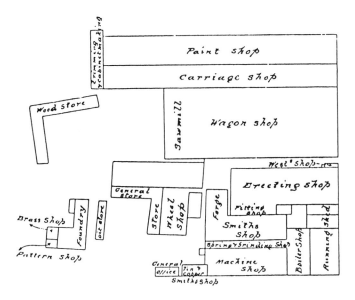

Cowlairs Works, floor plan about 1890.

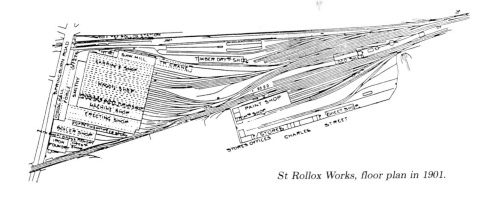

St Rollox Works, floor plan in 1901.

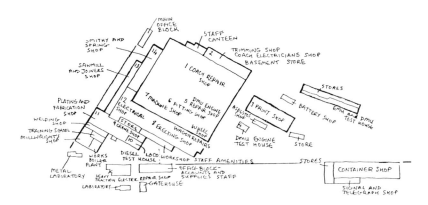

St Rollox Works, floor plan about 1970.

BRABY'S IMPROVED TIMBER AND IRON BUILDINGS.

TEA HOUSE.

Buildings for Tea or Rubber Factories prepared and shipped promptly.

A page from Braby's catalogue of about 1900.

BRABY'S
IMPROVED TIMBER AND IRON HOUSES.

TELEGRAPH STATION BUILDINGS,
BUNGALOWS, HOSPITALS,
HUTS, MOTOR GARAGES, ...
SHEDS AND BUILDINGS . . . . .
of every description supplied promptly.

DESIGNS AND ESTIMATES
PREPARED QUICKLY. . . . .

Board of Management for Glasgow Northern Hospitals

Foresthall Hospital
Glasgow

Training School for Enrolled Nurses

This Certificate is awarded to

Isabella L. Nelson.

who has trained here for two years

and has proved to be an efficient Nurse by

Written and Oral Examinations

and by Practical Work in the Wards

M. MacKinnon. ___Matron

R.G.H. Cunningham ___Medical Superintendent

Date ___DECEMBER 1964

Isa Nelson's Enrolled Nurses Certificate, 1964.

2

WORKERS ORGANISATIONS: CO-OPERATIVES & TRADE UNIONS

WORKERS' ORGANISATIONS — CO-OPERATIVES AND TRADES UNIONS

In the middle of the nineteenth century, the principle of workers using their combined strength to counteract the economic power of employers was not accepted in law or by individual employers. Workers therefore usually expressed their aims in terms of mutual self help, rather than in terms of conflict with their employers. The earliest organisation recorded in the Springburn area is the Keppoch Hill Friendly Society, formed in 1841 by coal miners. We know nothing of the society's later history but its surviving handwritten rules give us an insight into living and working conditions at the time when Springburn was about to be transformed by the opening of the Edinburgh & Glasgow Railway and the Cowlairs Works. The author begins with a vision of an ideal society where spontaneous help of those in need would be the norm:

'Is there anything to a man like a friend in need? And what characterizes him with a more distinguished mark of superiority than a heart of Liberality? It is the grace of his bosom while he lives, the immortalizer of his memory when gone, it suffers with the sufferer and rejoices with the prosperous, it is the friend of necessity, the life of the indigent, it is a world of munificence, where hands are compassion, where surface is honesty, atmospheric by benevolence, whose meliorating aims are the drops of philanthropy, and whose salutary revolution is on the axle of humanity. Were such an uniform and prevailing dispostion in man, there would be no necessity for flying to the partiality of societies as the whole family of man would be one great and grand society, but alas! it is not so.'

The harsh realities of a miner's life are quickly brought into the picture to explain why the society is necessary. His descriptions of the evils which make societies necessary are graphic and biting:

'One has become the sordid extortioner, another the insatiable monopolizer, the avaricious taskmaster and the contractee dotard — these all concur in their aggrandizement at the expense of oppressing the masses. Never ceases the urgent utility of forming ourselves into societies of this kind that by small remittances such a friend has accumulated and perpetuated as shall enable said society in same measure to supply the wants of the suffering member or in the event of death the surviving relatives.'

As well as their economic disadvantages, miners worked in such a hazardous profession that other friendly societies were unwilling to carry the risk of insuring them:

'What also ought take a double incentive in the dangers of our avocation so much indeed doth it appear even to the public that some

22

societies will not admit of us as members, and is it to be wondered at?' The author goes on to speak of the 'humiliating effects of our appaling (sic) employ' which 'cry aloud & demand us to establish such an institution as may, by good order and economic management, prove useful to all... Animated by these concerns, a number of persons at the Keppoch Hill Colliery did upon the first day of February 1840 form themselves into a society under the title of the "Keppoch Hill Friendly Society".'

The purposes of the society were defined as:

'First—to provide an aliment for members who may be rendered unfit for their employment in consequence of sickness or infirmity or accidents, provided always that one or more of these conditions have not been brought on by drunkenness or by fighting.

Second—to provide payment of a sum of money at the death of members, their wives or children as funeral money, and to these two purposes inclusive of the necessary expenses for management the whole fund shall be devoted.'

Membership was open only to those of 'good moral character' who were free of 'bodily trouble', who had a 'visible means of supporting himself' and who were between 15 and 45 years of age. Members' sons between 10 and 15 could become half members. This age range reflects use of child labour and the shorter life expectancy of the period. Members between 16 and 25 years paid three shillings entry money, those between 26 and 35 paid three shillings and sixpence and between 36 and 45, four shillings. Thereafter, they paid sixpence a fortnight. Members claiming 'aliment' were visited by two of the Society's managers. If they judged the claim justified, the member got seven shillings a week; if they were doubtful, a certificate was sought from a surgeon, at the invalid's expense. After 12 weeks, the aliment was reduced to five shillings, and to three shillings after 24. The latter involved putting the invalid on the superannuation list and he continued to receive his three shillings 'so long as their indisposition & the Society shall last'. The daughters of members only received their benefit if they were free of 'church scandal'.

In the following decades, friendly societies providing similar benefits were founded in Springburn, including the Hyde Park Locomotive Works Friendly Society, Ancient Order of Free Gardeners, and Ancient Order of Foresters, the Independent Order of Rechabites, the Oddfellows, and the Irish National Foresters. These bodies, organised and run by the workers themselves, provided the only systematic help in time of hardship, apart from the provisions of the poor law and religious charities. The ability to contribute a regular sum to a friendly society from a small wage required careful management, and all the societies placed great emphasis on respectable behaviour and on temperance in particular. Death or illness of a breadwinner who was too poor or disorganised to pay a friendly society membership would have severe consequences for his dependants. Even a slight lapse from the straight and narrow could result in him and his family being deprived of their benefits. Thus thrift and morality were closely linked. Many of the friendly societies owned halls which served as social centres as well as meeting places and they continued to play a key role in supporting the individual and the community until they were superseded by the Welfare State after the Second World War.

Co-operatives

While it was rare for workmen to be able to set up in manufacturing on their own because of the great capital cost, they were able to take on the distribution of goods through co-operatives. The earliest co-operatives were the Petershill and Keppochhill Co-operative Societies, both founded in the 1860s. The best known and most successful was the Cowlairs Co-operative Society, which was founded in 1881 by a group of North British Railway employees who met in the Cowlairs canteen. In the early days, it was managed on a voluntary basis by NBR men and it quickly became the largest retail organisation in Springburn. So successful was it in fact that a group called the Traders' Protective Association approached the NBR management asking that they dismiss any employee involved in running the co-op. The six North British men on the board duly received notices. The community, including doctors and ministers as well as their fellow workers were outraged, and the notices were withdrawn after a meeting between the general manager of NBR and Mr (later Sir) William Maxwell of the Scottish Wholesale Co-operative Society. (John Thomas, 1963, pp 124/125.) By the 1950s, the co-op had over a hundred branches and had spread to Bishopbriggs and Kirkintilloch, Robroyston, Possilpark and Lambhill. It provided for every conceivable need from coal to baby clothes, from meat and fish to gravestones and played a key role in the community. Everyone over a certain age remembers their co-operative share number and the dividend or *divi* was often the largest sum families had at any one time. The unemployment which accompanied the decline of the railways and other industries, the changes in retail organisation and the movement of people out of Springburn, as a result of the Overspill Policy, undermined the co-operative's base. It gradually contracted and finally closed down in the early 1980s.

Trades unions

Friendly Societies and co-operatives were positive initiatives by workers to take control of parts of their own lives without directly coming into conflict with employers. Friendly societies were approved of or at least tolerated by employers, as they assumed responsibility for sick or injured workers. Thus, the Hyde Park Locomotive Works Friendly Society was formed in 1863, the year after the works were established. This promptness, and the introductory paragraphs of the rules may indicate that it was actually an employer or management initative:

'As it is desirable that the working classes should, wherever practicable, form Societies for providing for themselves during periods of sickness or in case of death, the workmen of Messrs Neilson and Company, Hyde Park Locomotive Works, Springburn, with that object constitute this Society on 23 February, 1863.'

Direct negotiation with the employers over wages and conditions however, was clearly a major area of potential conflict. The degree of conflict varied from one firm to another. Neilson was in many ways a typical nineteenth century paternalistic employer, who liked to think of himself as being benevolent to his workers. While he might approve of a friendly society, he would disapprove strongly of a trades union, and the Hyde Park management remained strongly anti-union right up to its closure. As a private company, it had a different relationship with its workers than the more impersonal atmosphere in the Cowlairs and St Rollox Works, which were parts of large national companies with huge traffic departments.

In the last quarter of the nineteenth century, competition between the railway companies increased, and they attempted to cut costs by forcing the engine drivers and guards to work longer and longer hours. They were supposed to work a 144 hour fortnight, but in practice, this was a minimum, as compulsory overtime steadily increased. Professor James Mavor of Glasgow University surveyed working conditions and found that one crew on a freight run to Edinburgh had worked 21, 21, 19, 19, and 24 hours on five consecutive days. Another crew worked 17, 16, 18, 24 and 15 hours over a five day period, and averaged 17 hours a day for a month. The men finally cracked and in December 1890, a Scottish national strike was called. It was initially successful, but even after the companies lost much public sympathy for evicting strikers from company houses in Motherwell, the men did not have the resources to hold out, and there were too many unemployed willing to take the jobs. Though most of the workers got their jobs back, they always took second place to the '1890' men when it came to promotion. (John Thomas, 1963, p. 152/153.) An account of events during the strike in the Glasgow Herald of 31 December 1890 seems to imply that both departments were on strike:

'Disturbance at St Rollox—Arrest of a fireman

At St Rollox the night did not pass off as peacefully as at Polmadie.

There was a much larger picketing party on duty than on any of the previous nights, although, so far as the police are aware, there were very few outsiders among the number. That is to say the duty was performed by railway men, and not to any appreciable extent by members of other trades, some of whom seem to be more inclined to favour a policy of physical force. However that may be, a slight disturbance took place and the glass in a signal-box on the North British lines was smashed. Superintendent Colquhoun of the St Rollox division was in command of fifty constables, but as the ground he had to cover is very extensive, and includes both the Caledonian and North British lines, as well as the goods depots at Cowlairs and Sighthill, his men were necessarily considerably scattered. For the greater part of the night, pickets walked about in companies of from four to eight, but in every case where it could be accomplished the little parties were broken up by the police. In no case was any resistance offered to the action of the constables, although the men lost no time in reforming themselves into groups. Shortly after midnight, a body of strikers, sixty strong, arrived upon the scene. They came up the High Street from the central district of the city, and proceeded in marching order in the direction of the railway at St Rollox. Such a formidable array of men naturally occasioned some anxiety, and the police determined to prevent their further progress. A sufficient number of constables having been rapidly got together the strikers were charged. This move on the part of the constables had evidently not been calculated upon, and without waiting to make even a show of opposition the men scampered off in all directions. About this time, the glass in a signal box on the North British line where it passes under Petershill Road was smashed. The crash was heard by several constables, who at once ran to the place. They met several railway men, whom they identified as men who had been acting as pickets. Other two men (sic) were seen running off in an opposite direction. The railway men, whose names and addresses are known, denied all knowledge of the outrage. There were four men on duty in the signal box at the time. On a search of the ground in the locality being made several pieces of brick were discovered, and it is believed that it was with these that the glass was broken. Later that morning a young man, who stated that he was a North British fireman, was arrested on a charge of disorderly conduct in Springburn Road. On being searched at St Rollox Police Station a number of large stones were found in his pockets. He was detained in custody.

'*3.15 a.m.*

The contrast with the conditions of affairs yesterday still continues, and at Polmadie all is still quiet, the arrangements of the police having been most effective. In the St Rollox district matters are also very quiet, and only a few pickets are to be seen wandering about. It appears that the charge against the North British fireman who was arrested in Springburn Road, mentioned above, is much more serious than that of mere disorderly conduct. As entered in the police books the prisoner is charged with a contravention of section 7 of the Conspiracy and Protection to Property Act, 1873, by heading a disorderly mob, and attempting to strike an engine fireman, while returning from his work, with a view to compelling him to abstain from work.'

There is no separate mention of the locomotive building workers, as opposed to traffic department workers, and it is not certain to what extent St Rollox and Cowlairs Works employees were involved in the strike. One modern railway historian states, with reference to Hyde Park, that 'at the end of the century there was considerable industrial strife resulting in widespread strikes. The relationship between management and workmen had always been good and where neighbouring works went on strike for better conditions and more money, Neilson men did not—there was no need to' (Lowe, 1975, p. 504). This seems to refer to the 1890–91 Strike, and it is true that there was no break in the production at the Hyde Park Works at this time. Surviving employees reveal a great loyalty to the company even to the present day, as well as testifying to the strongly anti-union attitude of the management.

The General Strike 1926

Memories of the General Strike in Springburn do not give a clear picture. Perhaps it would be more accurate to say that they give an accurate picture of the confusion of the time, when it must have been difficult for people on the spot to get an overview of the situation. One local man, Alex Martin, recalls that Springburn was 99% behind the strike (Martin, 1981). Other evidence modifies this view to some extent. A letter from the AEU organiser in Springburn, George Mitchell of 157 Petershill Road, to the District Secretary, Harry Hopkins survives. It is dated 15th May, three days after the end of the Strike:

'As Convener in Cowlairs Works I am sending you this report of our work during the strike. Prior to ceasing work I got various shops to hold meetings and appoint shop committees. This was carried out in every one except Turning Shop, which I hope will fall in line after we resume. A Mass Meeting of Shop committees was held and a policy outlined for action when strike took place and on Tuesday 4th May not a man entered but it took quite a lot of Picketing to keep it up and not one entered during the Strike. We are resuming work on Monday as per your wire and we have assurance from Manager that there will be no victimisation. I have been appointed to act on Executive of Works

Committee and it will be my endeavour to see that the organisation now in being will carry on.

There is one point I hope will get consideration and recommendation from D(istrict) C(ommittee) to E(xecutive) C(ouncil), that is, payment to our members of Strike Benefit. The N.U.R. were paying to men who only joined after they were actually on the street and I think that payment to our men would stop a good number of our men from going over to N.U.R.'

Again Hyde Park workers were less involved, judging from a strike report to the Central Strike Committee of The National Union of Vehicle Buildings:

'NB LOCO COMBINE Our members (Coachpainters) withdrawn, all other Trades at work including House Painters. The moral is easy to read.'

James Aitcheson was an apprentice in the accounts department of St Rollox at the time. During the strike he remembers:

'There was quite a number of men went into work. I myself was in working. And the amusing thing was the tenements opposite as you were coming out, the women used to be waving black stockings at you —you were a blackleg working. But at my age it didn't matter much in 1926. You went past the pickets in the morning, they didn't bother because you were considered just a boy. If there was a lot of pickets at one gate you could go in another gate, which a lot of men did. And you could also walk up the line and come out at St Rollox running sheds, if you wanted to. Oh, plenty of ways in if you wanted.'

Unions since 1930

Unions are seen by most of our interviewees as an important form of self-help. The thirties were a bad period for unions because of the disillusion which set in after the General Strike in 1926 and the high level of unemployment. David Walters remembers the changes clearly:

'The AEU wasn't very strong at that time. It started to get stronger after the war. I think it was because of the idle time we had in the 1930s, up until the war started. Everything was the same, there was hardly any work for the men in Springburn at that time. Hyde Park was running low, so was the Caley, so was Cowlairs, so was Braby's. They were bad times, the nineteen thirties, right up until the war started and everybody had to work then... They weren't bothered because when anybody came into a job the firm could apply anybody in any job, didn't matter who they were. There'd be about a hundred men looking for one job, same as there is nowadays.'

The boom which followed 1945, and the impetus given to collectivism by the experience of the war, generated widespread support for unions. There was an increased professionalism in negotiating on both sides, and the unions dealt with management whereas previously they had dealt mostly with foremen. It is clear from the interviews that the ability of a union to change things often depended on the expectations of workers inside a particular workplace itself, and that those expectations were shaped by traditions often inherited from the nineteenth century. Thus, for example, until the late 1940s, the main issue concerning unions was wages. Working conditions and health and safety matters were not a major issue, and workers quite often accepted both risks and a harsh environment as part and parcel of the job. Willie Dewar graphically illustrates the tolerance of traditionally poor conditions until a new union came to Hyde Park in the early 1950s:

'Hyde Park for many years was very steady but once they started building diesel electrics, the GEC crowd, the electricians were very strong on unions then and the conditions weren't suitable for them in Hyde Park because these big doors up here [erecting shop] were always open at the yard. I should say into the yard, because all the wind blew in there and it's quite cold in the erecting shop. Although they had heating, the big doors had quite a few spaces, and then of course your uptakes had more spaces, and there were a lot of strikes when the electrical people came in to work with the mechanical people.'

Sanctions against union delegates

Employers were wary of the strength of unions to the extent that they took action against their leaders. Various sanctions were applied, chiefly loss of promotion, but if this failed to have the desired effect, dismissal and blacklisting could follow. This was complemented by the recruiting system, which worked by applying an informal network of selective patronage among families known to be dependable workers. The Hyde Park Works retained the family firm, anti-union atmosphere right up to the end. Willie Dewar remembers:

'Trade Unions were pretty strong latterly, but in my early days you didn't have meetings in the works. That was, all meetings were held outside. In fact if someone saw one of their men taking a spokesman's point at one of the meetings out in the vacant ground behind NB, then he'd been seen—that was his promotion chances shelved, because he was taking part in a union.'

Cathy Page's father, Joe Sweeney, was victimised soon after he returned to work after fighting and being wounded in the First World War. He was a tool-setting foreman at Braby's before the war, and came back to the same job. Whether or not his time in the trenches had radicalised him can only be guessed at, but it did give him a shock of white hair that made him easy for employers to identify. He later joined the Communist Party, became head of the National Unemployed

Workers' Movement in Springburn, and in his later years successfully trained to become a psychiatric nurse:

'It was practically unheard of for somebody in his position, who was a foreman, to bring people out on strike. And this is why he was so thoroughly distrusted. My father, as I say, came back from the First World War, and after he started in his trade union activities, he was made unemployed, simply because of his trade union work. That got you blacklisted in those days. Because you were a troublemaker if you were organising the people, trying to get trade unionism established in the early days, and he was regarded as a trouble maker.'

John Wotherspoon had a similar experience after returning from a time in New Zealand, where he had gone partly because of the slow rate of progress in achieving the union's ambitions before 1960:

'When I came back it was the hardest thing I had trying to get a job back in Cowlairs. Oh you were not on, because my past record was following me, you know. They were actually looking for men and word got round "Don't start him", you know. And I came up for interview. A bloke arranged with one of the foremen, he says they're looking for a marker off in the machine shop, will you take the job... He got me an interview. The foreman went to get me a form to fill in to give me the job, that was it. Told not to start me. It was a year altogether when I came back from New Zealand before they started me. I was at a football match and I met another delegate and he says, "They're looking for men in the erecting shop, John." I says, "You're only wasting your time, they'll no start me." He says, "We're looking for men, I'll see the foreman." So he arranged an interview for me and I went and saw the foreman and he says, "Oh, it's you," he says, "I didnae know you by name," he says, "Are you prepared to work in the stripping shop?" I says "Aye". He says, "Right you are." I says, "Well, before you waste your time, when you go into that office for a form for me they'll no give you one." He says, "I'm the foreman, I'll get the form. You wait here".'

Apprentices' strikes

Often, for a union in a dispute, there was a thin line between success and failure, so that if even one of its demands in a dispute was met, it could be seen as a victory. Paradoxically, however, since one of the original intentions of a trades union was to protect craft status and privileges, apprentices would find themselves unrepresented by their union. This was not a matter of choice, rather it was a question of money, as George Ingram makes clear. Serving his time during the Second World War, he found himself better off on strike than he was in work. The remarkable support of the female labour force is also plain, which shows how resonant the apprentice's dispute was. Perhaps this is because some of the womens' own sons or brothers had experienced the same low rates of pay, while other youngsters of the same age group could earn higher wages, albeit as 'unskilled' labourers. Married women always budgeted for the whole family, a delicate exercise, and a boy's 'keep' made a big difference to just getting by, and having an extra breathing space:

'I was in my third year when we had this strike and we were out for a couple of weeks and I must say, while we were out on strike with me being attached ... I was now in the tool room of the Atlas works, in the shell factory, and there were two hundred women in each shift, night-shift and day-shift. And they were most generous to the apprentices, so much so that nobody ever wanted to go back to work because we were better off on strike! I never had so much money in all my life, these women were all contributing. They were all contributing tremendously and once we shared out the spoils to ... I forget, there must have been about a dozen apprentices in the Atlas and then there was about another eight or ten apprentices in the Mons and the Marne works. But the money we got then was terrific. We didnae want to go and it was good weather then so that meant you could go and play football and you were still getting loads of money, but eventually the management came up and they gave us quite big increases; I forget what the increase was but I think my wages went up to a pound a week or something. So that was really about ... it went from fourteen bob to a pound, it's about thirty per cent of an increase in fact. That must have been about 1941.

'I wasnae a member of any union, oh no. But we had ... it was organised by the AEU, the engineering workers. But the apprentices were so badly paid that somebody had to do it. They were the main instigators of chasing people up for a rise, the AEU, although as an apprentice, I wasn't in the AEU at all. In fact it was later on in my apprenticeship that I joined the AEU. After we got the rise we could afford to be in the AEU.'

Skilled journeymen, who were sometimes responsible for half a dozen apprentices at a time, shared the Atlas women's concern. They had, of course, already experienced the same unequal treatment as young men themselves. David Walters, now a janitor in Springburn College, was AEU secretary at Cowlairs:

'Oh, they were quite willing for the apprentices, because the apprentices were starting off with eleven and sixpence a week. Eleven and sixpence! They were hardly making two pounds a week when they were in their fourth year, and working the same machines as some of the tradesmen were working. Doing the same work as tradesmen and getting very poorly paid for it... They took the whip round for apprentices. My father and mother, they didnae bother about me being on strike. In these days it was only apprentices that had to pay digs or that, so, the journeymen had a whip round and that was for them to pay digs.'

Joseph Docherty, a fitter in St Rollox, was drawn into union activity by the injustices experienced by apprentices:

'The Caley was quite good up until I started taking a kind of interest in the union. I wasn't too bad an apprentice so that kind of saved you. If you were a dumpling I suppose your head was for chopping off. You see, boys weren't allowed on committees, which was an injustice. And at that time they were starting what they called the Bevin Ballot scheme. Ernest Bevin, who had been a Labourite, a great Labour man so-called, and he started doing this! I think he was doing his Ministry of Labour during the war. Well, he wasn't elected into the government, he was co-opted by Churchill because he was General Secretary of the Transport & General Worker's Union. And he started what they called the Bevin Ballot Scheme. Couldn't get miners, you know, people down the mines, so what happened? They had a ballot scheme, everybody's name of certain ages, maybe from sixteen to twenty, went in a hat, probably some kind of semi-twopence-ha'penny computer they had in those days, and if your name came out the hat, that was you down the pits.

'So, because of that, you were fighting, supposed to be, the boys that were in the army were fighting against Fascism! One of their big things was direction of labour, that they decided where you could work and we're fighting this. So our argument was that they were going to dictate to us where we were working, how you'll go. I mean everybody knew there had to be certain regulations for the war, but to stick a boy that was in the middle of his time down the pits, and I mean you were going down there as a miner, you weren't going down as a fitter. It was a terrible waste.

'So we had boys from all over the Clyde area. We used to have a committee called the Clyde Apprentices Committee, and the railway had never been a part of it, but this kind of united everybody, all the apprentices on the Clyde. And another boy and I, big Bob, I think he's still with the railway. I think he's a Superintendent now, so he'll not want to be quoted, but him and I were elected delegates for the Caley and we went to most of the meetings and that against the Bevin Ballot Scheme. And eventually we decided we'd go on strike, you know. Going on strike during the war was illegal, you couldn't go on strike, but we did. I can't remember how long we were out, a few weeks. When you become one of those delegates you're either going to be bought off, it's not so hard to do with a boy. Just offer him a couple of good wee jobs and good things ... I didn't fancy that.

'I pestered them right enough, I wanted to volunteer to go into the army, which was pretty stupid, but I was about eighteen, nineteen at the time, I just don't remember. But they wouldn't let you go because you were in a protected occupation, the railway was a grade one protected occupation. Reserved Occupation they called it. And so eventually they sent for me and said they would give me my release and let me go to the army, so I found myself in the army. That was only because, I think, you were doing your delegate, you know.

'And then you were married, you know, you had to toe the line more. They've got you economically then, I suppose. I didn't do much in NB, although between, before I went to NB and after it, well I did, when I was in the fabrication shop, I was a kind of, I don't know what you'd call it, it was a kind of sub-convenor for the Atlas works. But the Atlas works were only half works then, you know, and I was a shop steward and by then it wasn't really, it didn't even look like a relative of NB Loco, you know, the big erecting shops were shut, the cranes were dismantled.

'When we were on strike we ran a big dance, just actually what brought my mind to orchestras! We had a thirteen-piece orchestra, you know, half of them apprentices and half of them other guys... It was Joe, I think, that organised our orchestra for the Springburn Public Halls, and we had our dance in there to collect funds to pay the boys. Some boys, apprentices, were married young. That's what you called the hardship cases, you know. You had to get money to pay them. We ran other things too. Used to pay them out, pay the boys out, and there used to be a football park opposite the Caley, the Huntington. The Hunts they called it. And we got a loan of their, it wasn't a pavilion, it was just a bloody big hut, and we paid out our money in there, you know. Hardship, real hardship cases. I know a boy, I'll no' mention his name, because it wouldn't be fair, he was married and had a couple of youngsters, just as a young boy. So he got his full wages, just paid him his full wages. Other boys that, if there was a lot of people maybe widowed, and that was their son, you know, their son was working with us, they were kind of their mother's sole support, you gave them their full whack. Other boys maybe their mother was a widow but they had sisters working, well, they got a percentage, you know. It was well organised. Aye, it taught you good things.

'I remember one time barring the *Daily Express*. I don't know how many boys we had in the Caley, but there was hundreds of apprentices there. There was squads that was nothing else but apprentices, some of the fitting shop squads had nothing else but apprentices. And we had a big meeting down in the Christian Institute in Bothwell Street, and the day before, when the big strike happened, there was thousands out, thousands of boys out. But the *Daily Express* printed a wee bit about three hundred boys out on strike, as they always do, play things down. So, I was doing my door steward. The committee's idea was bar the

Express 'til they print a retraction, and when the *Express* came, I said, "You're not getting in." "Aw, come on, let us in, we're just earning a living an' a'." Course that's the story they give you, then they stab you in the back and print a lot of lies. So we said, "Aye, when you print a retraction of the three hundred, and make it more realistic."

'So I mean, although you were only a boy, the training we had from some of the boys that had been involved in strikes, there was a thruppence an hour strike years before it, and a lot of that committee were still boys, though older, and other ones were tradesmen, who gave the boys guidance, I mean they were really well organised, you know. So it gave you a good grounding for trade unionism and your politics. We created such a fuss—our strike was unsuccessful, by the way—we didn't win the Bevin Ballot scheme. They kept it, but what we did was, we won recognition in the Caley, for the boys. We were allowed to represent the boys from then on. Not at big meetings, you couldn't approach the management, but what you could do, you had a watching brief as they called it, you sat in with the men that held the works committee, you had your say. But any representation was done by men and most of the men in it were all bloody right-wingers anyway!'

Divisions among the workers

The effectiveness of unions was dependent on unity among the shop floor workers. The most damaging divisions were those between skilled and unskilled, and between Catholic and Protestant. John Wotherspoon saw them both as a threat to the objectives of trades unionism and worked to diffuse them:

'In Cowlairs we had a right bad period we went through, and it was the background of one man that caused the whole thing, the Billy and Dan stuff you know... There was all sorts of accusations against him in the works that he was getting Catholics started, all this type of thing, that he was starting the men and not the staff clerk, and that it was Roman Catholics he was starting.'

The incident blew up into a libel court case which badly affected relations in the works for a time. In general, however, Mr. Wotherspoon didn't see it as a major factor in the life of the works:

'I wouldn't say it was a big issue. Springburn was pretty well mixed. You had the pockets of Protestants and pockets of Catholics and when you get these pockets you maybe get people who try to use them. You'll always have people in the workshops who try to use Freemasonry and Catholics and organisations, but where we seen it taking place in the works committee, we always tried to smash it right away and tried to get the people to dissociate themselves from anything of this character, but they used it for their own ends.

'We argued that at one time you could have tradesmen working in a shop getting a bonus, and you could have a labourer, he didn't get any bonus and yet he was labouring to the squad of men that were making the bonuses. Well, we eventually argued to embrace everybody in the bonus systems, and everybody should get the same percentage on their different rates... It was amazing the difference it made to cranemen and slingers and ordinary labourers in the workshops when they got the bonus attached to the skilled worker they were working with, because they were contributing to the efforts that were made. Well, management werenae happy about it. They tried all sorts of schemes to try and leave these other workers out, but eventually we fought and got them embraced in the same schemes.'

Recruiting the unskilled

Outside of industry, some sectors of working life were historically barren for organised labour. This was true of the so-called service sector and especially so in hospitals. Working traditions there emphasised the importance of received behaviour and 'knowing your place.'

Helen Woods was a domestic nurse in Stobhill Hospital and a dedicated trade unionist all her life. She demonstrates the effect one committed individual can have on a large established institution:

'I went down to finance and I said to him, "Is there no' a union in this hospital?" He said, "Don't mention unions 'cause you'll be right out the gate." I even said that when I was being presented as a nurse and I said, "Oh, will I?" So I says, "I'll join a union and that's that." So I went back to the ward and I told the sister in charge about it. She said, "We're not even allowed to join a union." I says, "Right." So somebody must have told this man and my own husband was in the union as well, not in Stobhill. And this day I was coming off duty at twelve o'clock and this man was outside the gate in Stobhill and he says to me, "'Scuse me, you Helen Woods?" And I said, "Aye, I think so." "Well," he said, "I'm led to believe you want to join a union," and I said, "Oh, yes." He said, "Well, I'll be up once a fortnight and I'll take your subscription." I said, "Oh, fair enough then, that suits me."

'And he gave me a wee yellow card and I think I gave him a shilling. It was a shilling—if it wasn't a shilling it was ten pence—and he marked my card and that was me a member of the G & M. And I said to him, "I'm in the union." He says, "That's good." He was the secretary, he said, "Let me see your card." I was in the same union as my man was in, and my man could have joined me in it. And the man that joined me was one of my old neighbours, Paddy Harrity. Paddy Harrity was the one that joined me. Now today, if you don't get a job, if you're lucky enough to get one in Stobhill, you'll not get into it unless you join a union. And that's through me.

I told them, [fellow workers], I said, "Get into the union, get in."
Because there was a lot of grievance there and they couldnae get
nothing done without being a member of the union. Particularly on
your knees with a big brush and that. I'm talking about domestic, I'm
not talking about the nursing, I wasnae asked to do anything like that
but that wasn't my point. These women were on their knees and they
shouldnae have been on their knees. And big corridors on your knees.
So we brought in officers and we got it organised into a union, a
hundred per cent union.'

Negative views

Negative attitudes towards trades unions range from the frustration of
former activists to the scepticism of people who had never believed.
Joseph Cairns, formerly a 'Barra' painter in Hyde Park, is disillusioned
after a life-time of struggle on behalf of his fellow workers:

'I did my shop steward and that, and I had to fight like hell for to get
the conditions for everybody else. It didnae do me much good. Wish I
hadnae bothered now. I finished up and I came home from the war, I
started again. I did my chairman in the AEU in a branch we had up in
the church (hall) at Queenshill. There was a lot of strikes. For all the
good it done, a waste of your time. I was in organised strikes in
Cowlairs. It's a waste of time but.'

Dick Johnstone, a cable worker in Flemington House, Craigpark
Cable Works, is also sceptical of unions. To him, they seem like self-
interested bureaucracies:

'Transport & General Workers. Not that I wanted to be, I didn't like
unions. You've got to be ... it's blackmail. If you hadn't a union card
you wouldnae get started. I don't believe in unions. You paid it every
week... It would be about a shilling or one and six. You were supposed
to get it if the strike was official, but I never heard of anything being
official. In other words you were paying it for bugger-all, because if they
had to pay money they made it unofficial.'

Martha MacMillan was a tracer in Hyde Park Works, and in many
ways was a typical Hyde Park worker in that trade unions were really
an irrelevance to her. Her loss of wages occurred just as she was able
to save for the first time, and she demonstrates the sense of unfairness
which can arise when a dispute involves people with no personal
grievance or commitment to union values. However, the union's
defence of her sole right to practise her craft is revealed:

'I'm not really union-minded. Oh, I'll never forget it, the only strike
I was ever involved in. We had plenty of work and no complaints as far
as I knew. Maybe the union members had, but Swan Hunter in New-
castle were on strike. So what they did was pinpoint a firm that had a
lot of work and it would damage them if they brought them out on

strike. And that's what they did with us. We went in in the morning to start our work as usual and, our office was like the stairs of a ship, and I looked up and here's this man standing at the top and he says to me, "Are you a member of a trades union?" And I said, "Yes." He said, "What's your name?" He says, "Read that." Of course what had to be read would have taken all day. He says, "I'm sorry but you've no work. You're out on strike." Now we left our boards and tracings partly done, and believe you me, we went back and that tracing was still there, they wouldn't dare touch it. But we were out for eight weeks, and what angered me was the men had their wives out working, so they had an income coming in, you see they stopped money for us, we got nothing. But they had their wives working with an income or if it was a wife out the husband was working. I was on my own and I had nothing. All they allowed us was three-quarters our basic wage. Now our basic wage wasn't much because it was the extras that brought it up. So it means that that was the year I was going to America on holiday, I had never been abroad in my life and it was of great effect of fairness on me. And I was saving as hard as can be and here I was knocked out, no money.'

As unions became more powerful, their own management network came under closer scrutiny from the shop-floor, because it was felt that some unions tended to repeat, in the workers' eyes, the employers' own management failures, including patronage and incompetence. Any deduction from a working wage was important, especially so if the donor could see no obvious return for his money. A union's suspected misuse of funds was always keenly felt, however apocryphal the allegations. Fred Holmes, a railway labourer, resented both these aspects of organised labour:

'The chap who collected the money in my lot spent it on booze, so that quite a lot of men who'd been paying union dues were in the union's bad books. The one period when the unions, they call them union bosses, well the bosses were just like the management. It got so that you couldnae get working overtime without the permission of the secretary of the works' committee. And I was told I was eighteen months in arrears with my payments, my union dues like, and I always paid in advance, two or three months in advance and everybody knew. This fella had pinched the money, and the union must have known it from the past record that I was never in debt to the union, but he sent for me to accuse me of being eighteen months... This fellow had been stealing the money all the time, but as I say, they knew the kind of fella he was and all these men put in all their payments at one time, because he drank in the same pub as the works' committee. He did one of the old pals' acts, you see? And that was common, money was pinched.'

Henry Stewart, a heating engineer, holds what might be regarded as a typical view of what trades unions meant for the average worker at

E

a time when there was a consensus about their role in the workplace. He associates them with both apprenticeships and restricted entry to a firm. He also perceives the value of trade unions in being able to negotiate wage structures, which were more far-reaching than just wage rises, and represented the sharing of a management decision. The fact of unions negotiating with employers on a more equal basis is a product of the recent past. Note also the stage in his career when he leaves the union:

'The Heating and Ventilating Domestic Engineer's. And at that time when you served your time you really had to be in a union. It was pretty tight, and if you didn't hold a union card you couldn't work in the heating trade. That was basically the thing and I joined the union in my first year and I was right in until I was in the office. Until I got a collar and tie on, I was always in the trade union... The good thing at that time was the union and the employer, although they have been very close in the heating trade, the employers have always been very close with the unions, they have always had a straightforward agreement: every year, they get a rise. A wee bit haggling here but generally speaking, yes. The answer is, it was a closed union. You couldn't really work in the heating trade if you weren't in the union, and it did help your wage structure.'

The nationwide decline of heavy industry, coming after the postwar boom when men were doing 'two nights and a Sunday' overtime, demoralised the workforce, and consequently affected their attitude to trades unions. Between 1954 and 1966, Springburn suffered a net loss of between 8000 and 9000 jobs in manufacturing industries (Corporation of Glasgow, Glasgow University, nd, para. 4.6). Unions had grown up in response to a particular type of industrial structure. After a period of relative stability in the system, it began to change rapidly and extensively from the late 1950s. This put the unions under great pressure to keep up and to defend hard-won rights which were now labelled as restrictive.

John Wotherspoon strongly rejects the charge that union intransigence was the cause of the decline of industry:

'They highlight the demarcation, you know, the twang of the string and all that sort of stuff. That wasn't created by the unions. They themselves, the employers, created these positions first, because they wanted to have all the different skills in the factories and they want to have the apprenticeships. The apprenticeships was a good thing for the employers, but as far as we were concerned, it was cheap labour. So, whenever we became a journeyman we had to protect what we were serving our time for. And that's all the men were doing, protecting their trade.

'An awful lot of the strikes that you did hear of in the Clyde and places like that were provoked to put the men on the street and show how ridiculous were the working agreements inside that factory, instead of getting the works committee and hammering and hammering out until they got an agreement. Our working practices changed an awful lot in the railway industry. We had strict demarcation lines, but when it was necessary, the one thing I can safely say, before a man went out of that door redundant we had to look at every aspect of how we could absorb him, and if it meant changing certain practices in our trade we changed them... Some trades weren't just interested. The electricians is a bad lot to try to deal with, you know. They'll take nobody into their trade, but the other trades, most of them, we could get an agreement with them, and I can safely say that out of all the men that have left the whole industry we've had a choice for them, to go into another trade or go out the door.'

From the vantage point of the 1980s, many interviewees, retired or enduring the extended retirement of the redundant over-50's who will never work again, are influenced as much by the present situation as by unions' past achievements. Improvements in wages and conditions are quickly absorbed and taken for granted. However, the unions are in a relatively weak position when it comes to defending their members against closure of either commercial or nationalised factories. David Walters still remembers vividly the closure of Associated Electrical Industries (formerly Metropolitan-Vickers).

'It closed down the AEI, in Petershill Road. It used to be the old Denmores', and the AEI took it over. I was years there and then it closed down. Made redundant out of there ... because they were going short of work ... over to Larne in Ireland, they took the work away from the wee factory in Springburn.'

Campbell Christie, General Secretary of the STUC, sees this kind of decision-making as being one of Springburn's central problems:

'I think the instincts that say that we don't need to be a nation depending on services, depending on taking in each other's washing, are right. We've got the legacy of skill and the capacity. When you reflect on it, what happened was we had bad management, I mean, industry had bad management. North British was an example—one only assumes looking back that the management didn't at an early enough stage take decisions about the future, they were concerned about the present ... the same with the railway. You get angry because you had all the railway works there, but what happened is, because of the decision-making being taken away from Scotland, a corporate decision from the British Railway boards closed St Rollox two years before it was ever announced it was closed. But they had decided it was going to close, because they decided they weren't going to invest in it; they were going to concentrate their repair and manufacture in Doncaster and Crewe and places like that. So, what makes you angry is you see all these things and you say, we could do things differently, we shouldn't accept that you just leave it to the market and it will happen. If you leave it to the market, it won't happen. It's happened to a lot of industries throughout Glasgow and Scotland. I mean, there are some good ones where you've got good management, but it all boils down to having proper plans or having a perceptive management.'

In many respects, the defensive nature of trades unions limits their range of action at a time of rapid economic change. Their ultimate weapon—the withdrawal of labour—is not very effective if the management, influenced by macro-economic factors and remote from the workplace, decides on closure. In view of the rapidity of the changes, the unions have in fact survived remarkably well, adapting more rapidly than many of the old industries within which they grew up, and still providing important support, both practical and psychological, for many members of the community.

David Hutcheson's membership certificate of the British Order of Ancient Free Gardeners Friendly Society, 1896.

North British Railway Strike Group 1890/91.

Membership Certificate of The United Society of Boiler Makers and Iron and Steel Ship Builders 'presented to Br. John Martin by the EXECUTIVE COUNCIL as a mark of their appreciation for past services to the Society and with a hope of further good work on the Society's behalf, 13/8/1910'.

John Martin, chief boilermaker in the St Rollox works.

Charles Clarkson's membership certificate of the Amalgamated Society of General Toolmakers, Engineers and Machinists. He began working as an indentured apprentice in the Hyde Park Works in 1906.

Charles Clarkson at 68 years of age.

A march from Springburn to George Square to protest against the closure of the Cowlairs Works.

Springburn families in the summer of 1984 protesting against the closure of the Glasgow (St Rollox) Works.

The BREL (St Rollox) Works Committee with banner, 1984. In the background are the Sighthill flats.

A National Council of Labour Colleges Certificate in Shop Stewards' Duties presented to Andrew Stuart, a member of the AEU. Mr Stuart worked in Metropolitan Vickers (later Associated Electrical Industries) in Petershill Road from 1953 to 1968.

3

APPRENTICESHIP: THE DOOR TO A JOB FOR LIFE

APPRENTICESHIP—THE DOOR TO A JOB FOR LIFE

Most boys had their first experience of paid work before they left school, delivering milk or messages out of school hours. Among Springburn's famous sons, both broadcaster and writer Tom Weir and tenor Sydney MacEwan recall this period of their lives with pleasure. Canon MacEwan's account is the most detailed:

'It was therefore a red-letter day in my life when the offer came from one of my pals whose name was Sanny Seton. "I'm gie'in' up the milk, dae ye wahnt the joab? I could put in a word wi' Grace at the dairy."

'Sanny was no ordinary milk-boy. He worked with the Co-op—and a Co-operative milk-boy had considerable status. There were only a dozen attached to our Cowlairs branch, and they were a respected elite —the cream of milk-boys in fact.

'Mother's reaction to my milk-boy suggestion was therefore initially chill. I told her the wage was three shillings a week—a fortune for a 12-year-old. We needed the money as much as the next one—but if the financial aspect impressed her at all, she certainly managed to conceal her enthusiasm. Remember, teachers in Catholic schools were paid very little before the 1918 Education Act—they were paid by the Church.

'It was only with a grudge that I got permission for Sanny to make the approach. Granny made the philosophical observation: "Sure he'll not likely get the job."

'But Grace, the woman in charge of the dairy, had known me for years and approved of Sanny's nominated successor.

'Not that such an appointment was filled as simply as that. My mother and I had to travel to the Cowlairs head office and fill in and sign all sorts of forms. No wonder there was pride in my heart when I set out into the grey of the dawn with my arms weighted down with tincans on my very first rake for the Co.

'A rake was a round, and the milk bottle hadn't been invented. I was allocated our own tenement, and five times between six and eight a.m. I had to run clattering back to the dairy for Grace to refill my cans.

'Up and down stairs in every close I stopped and gave each customer a can. And always it was a completely faceless operation. The can reappeared round the partly-opened door, sometimes on the end of a pale, naked arm. Even in Springburn, there was too much pride to be seen face to face at that early hour when the pallor and the wrinkles and the stubble of the night had not yet been erased. Modesty forbade that even a wee milk-boy should see a man in his nightshirt.

'I gave the three bob to my mother intact. That still left me in pocket. Every Saturday, for all their comparative lack of riches, some of the

42

good folk of Springburn gave me a ha'penny or a penny to myself. I felt like a millionaire.' (MacEwan, 1973, p 23–6.)

Joe MacKay had similar experiences around the same time and still remembers the effort and hazards vividly, nearly eighty years later:

'I'd say I was about eleven or twelve. I went around with papers. See, 6 o'clock in the morning wasn't new to me, because I was out at a quarter to six every morning for the Dairy opening. And I ran with milk too, to 8 o'clock, three big heavy rakes of milk down Wellfield Street and up three floors, bare feet, and when I was finished there—we stayed in Flemington Street at the time—I raced down into Ayr Street, to the wee paper shop, and I got the papers in there, and I delivered his papers, and then I went up the stair and got my school bag, and I had to run all the road, along Ayr Street, down Atlas Street, around Barcaple Street, Wellfield Street, up Anderson Street into Wellfield School, and I was in for 9 o'clock. And I worked on a Saturday in a butcher's shop in the Townhead, on a Saturday all day, at the mincing machine, going on messages. I went down on my bike, and I had a parcel of meat on my bike—he gave me a parcel of meat, which I thought was quite good, you know. One day I was just passing Charles Street and there was a big dog came after me. The meat was hanging on the handlebars ... I've still got the mark on my leg yet, the back of my leg, with the dog after me, and it grabbed me just at the leg there. One of his teeth went in right there, and I was dragging it—I couldn't get away from it. I think it was the meat... By the time I got home, my foot was full of blood, and I mind going to school, and I came back, and I was sent to go to the doctor, and he cauterised it. He took a wire or something, he put acid or something on it and he pulled it on a swab. I was sitting screaming.'

This type of work usually became full-time on leaving school at fourteen, as there was a minimum age of sixteen for beginning an apprenticeship. Alternatively, a boy might get a job as an office boy, rivet heater or forge hammer handler in a factory and proceed to an apprenticeship in the same works once he came of age. However, the crucial decision for a sixteen year old and his family was whether or not to go for an apprenticeship or become an unskilled labourer. In the family budget, any extra wage other than the father's was an important supplement, and could mean the difference between the family just keeping its head above water and the purchase of a few 'luxuries'. Between the first and last years of an apprenticeship, wages more than doubled. This is testimony not as to how generous wages became at the end of a boy's time, but rather to how meagre they were at the beginning. Apprenticeships meant comparative hardship for any family willing to forego the immediately higher wages their son could earn as an unskilled labourer. Thus patterns of either apprenticeships or unskilled labour tended to repeat themselves within families, from generation to generation. Those who were skilled were more likely to be able to call on a regular and higher wage than those who were unskilled, and could more easily subsidise the lower returns of the initial years of the apprenticeship. Jimmy Vaughan recalls his earnings when he began his apprenticeship in the St Rollox Works in 1923:

'When I first began my apprenticeship, you got five bob a week. That was your time rate. And then you got your piecework on top of that, which would be 100% and two and six war wage. This is something left over from the First World War. Total wages would be twelve and six. And then the second year, your basic went up to seven bob and then eleven and thirteen bob in following years. In your last year as an apprentice you'd be getting thirteen, plus maybe five bob. Finishing my apprenticeship I'd be getting about thirty shillings a week.'

Part of the attraction of apprenticeship was the security provided by the belief that workers would be able to practise the same skill for their whole working life, if not always in the same workplace, and in spite of periods of unemployment. John Wotherspoon left school during the Depression in 1935 and was unemployed for five months:

'Things were beginning to pick up but they werenae that you could just leave school and get a job. Oh I hawked all over. I walked down to the Clyde and walked here and walked there and couldnae get a job. People were always telling you they're starting boys here and starting boys there, and away you'd go. I was standing at the corner of Lenzie Street and Northcroft Road, and one of the teachers in the school came down, and she said "Are you no working yet?" I says. "No I cannae get a job," She says, "I'll see you here tomorrow same time, and I'll see what I can do for you". And the following morning I got a letter from Cowlairs to go down for an interview and I waited for her, and it was a job: I had to go for an interview in Templeton's Carpet place, it was someone she knew that was in the design place, and I wasnae too bad at designs in these days and she must have recommended me for a job. But when I told my mother and father at night, "I've to go to Templeton's and I've to go to Cowlairs for a job—what do I do?" "Go to Cowlairs, it's a job for life."'

Mr Wotherspoon became a fitter in Cowlairs, but before beginning his apprenticeship proper, like many boys he spent two years as an office boy: 'I learned a lot at that job. It was a great job. I was highly interested in it. It was ordering the materials for the works... You know the railways have a big contract out, and they had an inspection department and these inspectors used to go to the different places, up to Musselburgh, Brunton's and Wire Rope and all this sort of stuff, when they were buying steel plate from the steel works in Lanarkshire. I've been in them all. I used to go out with the inspectors, and hold the tape and his gauges and that and he checked all that material, that it was up to standard. Well I learned a lot and when the material was first being ordered for the departments—for the shops that was wanting it —they had what they called a requisition book, and this requisition came to us and I would look up the requisition book and get the drawings out for the particular material they were buying in, and often there was no reference to a drawing and I didnae know what they were wanting, and the bloke who was in charge of me would say, "Away down the shop, get more details o' that", and of course I made a lot of enemies of the foremen. They wouldnae know what information to give you. "Away out o' here." Of course this boss of mine, he done it more or less out of devilment to the foremen, making more or less sure they done their work, kind o' style. But I liked the job... It was amazing how much you learned in the job. You used to go home with a sore head, you know, I could never grasp it, but you gradually learned it and it was amazing the things I learned that came to my advantage in my life in the railways. I was using the knowledge I had learned as an office boy, you know.'

Most boys had far less interesting periods as office messengers, which may explain why Mr Wotherspoon felt more keenly than most the shortcomings of the apprenticeship system. Apprenticeship meant not only a job for life, but a skilled job, and this is what made the financial sacrifices worthwhile. He emphasises the distinction between skilled and unskilled labour inside the same workplace, and the role of apprenticeship in reinforcing it. However, in spite of his natural curiosity he saw night-school classes not as an opportunity for self-improvement, but rather as an evasion of the training responsibilities of management:

'Well, in those days, there's no doubt about it, it was only cheap labour. We actually done more labouring to the men than worked our apprenticeship. And that was always the thorn I had, every job I went to. I rebelled against labouring and I got into conflict with the foreman. I wouldnae push a barra and I used to try and get the other boys to do the same and on the last strike we got the decision taken and we stood by it until nobody would hurl barrows or any work that's called labouring work. In the erecting shop we'd only one labourer for each squad. You know it was ridiculous because the boys were doing everyday labouring, you know, about three quarters of their time would be labouring in the works, you know, and it was obviously no wonder it took you five years to serve your apprenticeship because you were wasting half your time labouring in the works instead of learning a trade like... During the period, I became the secretary of the apprentices committee and when we started our apprenticeship one of the conditions that was laid down to us was that we had to go to night school right until we were at least eighteen. I went to night school right through my apprenticeship, but I was one of the few. So I used to argue with the manager. I actually had numerous interviews with different managers on this point, on what they now call a day-release, getting some form of day-release for the boys. And it was my one constant argument with foreman and management during my apprenticeship: it was my right to get home at half past five and be finished with work. Any technical training I should be getting I should be getting in work somewhere... First and foremost I argued it on myself and then I gradually encouraged the apprentices' committee to think that way, that we shouldn't be going to night school. We should be getting some form of education. It was their duty to teach us any technical aspects of our trade, but some of the managers just laughed at you, you know? The idea of you wanting any technical training, you go to the night school and get it.'

For Douglas MacMillan, night school did not involve a compromise of principles, but the choice of whether or not to be ambitious: 'Night school was half expected in a way, because these things were taken into consideration from time to time, because maybe if you wanted a shift to the drawing office and that, these things were taken into consideration, but I never aspired to the drawing office.'

The apprentices' grievances concerning training and wages led to many disputes, which are dealt with in the chapter on Trades Unions. However, in small non-unionised workshops the apprentice who was dissatisfied with his training had only one weapon at his disposal. William Sancroft was the sole apprentice of a self-employed joiner:

'After we got all these potato baskets all built he told me to go and get a big barra, and he loaded the barra up and then he says, "Take this down to Tennant Street." I says, "I came here to learn the joinering trade, I didn't come here to do a horse out of a job". So he says, "Well, you take the barra out or you just put on your jacket," so I just put on my jacket.'

The division between the unskilled and the skilled created by apprenticeships was refined by divisions within apprenticeships. An apprentice attending night-classes, as well as proving his ambition, could make himself eligible for what were known as 'privileged' apprenticeships. These meant a greater knowledge of the whole workplace than those who had ordinary apprenticeships. For the latter, apprenticeships were still a symbol of respect, and picking up craft knowledge was a form of graduation. George Ingram had an ordinary apprenticeship, and John Menzies a 'privileged' one. George Ingram, first:

'Well, my apprenticeship was a five-year apprenticeship which started on my birthday in 1937, 20th December. And they had it organised that the apprentices in each department moved about to learn the various skills required within the department. Nowadays they move you about to various departments within a factory but in these days they only kept you within one department. For instance, I was in the erecting shop and we built or assembled railway engines, and the tenders which were two separate assembly units, they were built completely differently until they had to be put together to make an engine. So, within the apprenticeship you started on the cladding department. It's commonly called cladding where they cover the boiler with a thin plate of finished steel, sometimes it was a polished blue plate, it came up really lovely. My first job as an apprentice was to make these belts which held these plates in position, some of the belts were stainless steel, they were a polished stainless steel and we had to put belt ends on it, the belt ends were put on by riveting, so you had to learn the skill of marking holes, of punching holes and riveting, and when you riveted these belt ends on you had to make a very classy job of the rivets. Sometimes you had a snap-headed rivet where you had a special forming tool which gave it a nice sharp finish so that as well as being properly riveted it had to look nice as well. That was the first job in my apprenticeship. I joined another apprentice who was going to be moved onto his next position but he waited for another two or three days to show me how to do this particular operation, then he moved on. Well, eventually, after I had done a few months, I think it was about six months there, they moved us onto the tender squad where we built the locomotive tenders. But to get back to the cladding squad, I mean this was the place where we learned the initial skills of using a hammer and chisel and they had five fitters who used hammers and chisels all the time and they were very highly skilled people in the use of these. And they insisted that the apprentice learned to use it by fooling with that apprentice, kidding that apprentice on. They used to do tricks with hammers that you just wouldn't believe.'

John Menzies started work two weeks after his fifteenth birthday in the London, Midland and Scottish Railway Office in Buchanan Street, before moving on to St Rollox a year later. The day his apprenticeship ended was the last day in the existence of the LMS railway company. He saw out one era and the inauguration of another:

'I managed to get an apprenticeship in St Rollox works. The staff clerk in 302 Buchanan Street considered that the best place for people who were silly enough to want to become engineers. On 23rd March, 1942, I started in the toolroom. Not as a toolmaker or gaugemaker, but as the general dogsbody who had to keep the tool racks clean and see that the oil drums were filled up. That lasted about six weeks or so, then I was sent out to the Machine Shop where I was set to work, operating a Capstan lathe. This was in the critical period of the war. Now, apprentices were encouraged to, to use a phrase of the time, "improve

F

themselves", and they did this by going to evening classes. One was
encouraged to do this by being allowed to stop work half an hour early
at night, that was half past five, instead of six o'clock, and actually to
be paid for this! [The time off, not the classes]. You must bear in mind
that there were hundreds of apprentices in the works, and, I suppose,
in Glasgow there must have been thousands of apprentices at that time.
There was a population inhabited these evening classes. Trains were
full of people with T-squares and rolls of drawing paper and all the rest
of it. In St Rollox at that time, and before I arrived, they had, however,
set in place a form of apprenticeship training. They had a system
whereby the apprentices were moved around the works to various parts
of the works in order to get a broad experience of the trade and of the
work done. I'm referring now especially to apprentice fitters, turners,
coppersmiths, brass finishers. Others had similar, but necessarily more
restricted, movement in the works. There was an Apprentice Training
Manager, Mr Hunter, who had been a draughtsman in the St Rollox
drawing office, and he arranged for the transfer of all apprentices
throughout the works. You can understand that they couldn't move all
the apprentices on the one day, it would be quite chaotic, so he had to
arrange that people moved in batches, as it were. One stayed in a squad
or section for about three months, by which time it was considered that
you should have picked up the rudiments of what went on there. This
was in full operation when I arrived in St Rollox, and it was still in
operation when I left.

There was two types of apprenticeship for fitters. There was the
standard fitters' apprenticeship, and they introduced, some time before
I got there, an Engineering Apprenticeship, which was offered to boys
who had reached a certain degree of proficiency at the evening classes.
I got one of these apprenticeships after about two years. The difference
was that the boys in the Engineering Apprenticeship were given addi-
tional experience over what the fitters had. The engineering apprentices spent time in the iron foundry, learning how the moulders set
about their work; with welders; in the boiler shop, in addition to
working on the boiler mountings. And also we spent a period, up to
about six months, in a motive power depot. This was considered to
broaden our view of things. Of course, both the fitters and the engineering apprentices were left pretty much to their own devices in how much
they learned by themselves. They were given the opportunity, and it
was up to them to make of the apprenticeship what they could. There
was quite a number of men who took an interest in the boys. I recall
Harry Erskine at the surface table was interested in ensuring that the
boys learned to do the job properly. Albert Steven, in the fitting shop,
Jim Forsyth the chargehand, Jim Mitchell, the leading hand of the
motor squad, and Willie Lindsay, fitter in the motion squad, Jimmy

Airth who was on the pumps and the eccentric straps: those men did take an interest in the apprentices. But the apprenticeship was pretty wide in its scope, and looking back on it now, over the years, I could see, comparing it with what's gone on in other works in other towns in other countries, it wasn't too bad at all. In fact, for its time it would be just about as good as what was going. Engineering classes included Mechanics, Engineering Drawing, Thermodynamics, Applied Electricity, Mathematics, of course, Theory of Machines, General Design: all leading to Higher National Certificates or Higher National Diplomas. Also, once I'd finished the HNC, I took a course in Industrial Administration, which completed the examinations for membership of the Institute of Mechanical Engineers. [Examples of work done as an apprentice]: 'In the tender Shop, for example, bedding in wheel bearings, putting up cheeks for the axleboxes, hanging brake gear, putting up brake cylinders, drag boxes, and assembling the tender frame, anything attached to the tender frame. The boilermakers attended to the tank, but everything attached to the frame, water pick-up gear, and the water valves on the front end of the tender, flexible pipes for brake pipes and train heating pipes, that sort of thing, it was regarded as being a bit rougher than the engine work, which in its turn was regarded as being rougher than the fitting work. But it was all very necessary.'

John Wotherspoon recalls an incident which revealed the possible consequences of a narrow apprenticeship:

'This boy didnae know where any other shop lay in the works. He knew the way into the wagon shop and the way out into Cowlairs Road; that was all he knew. If he passed through a shop he knew that was the erecting shop, but what worked in it or what they done he didnae know. So he heard this argument about the painters painting boats, and it was the first or second meeting he was at, so he never said anything. He didnae take part in the discussion. And the following morning he says to the other bloke that was his delegate, "Hey Jimmy," he says,, "What?" "Going to take us over to the paint shop?" He says, "What d'ye want to go to the paint shop for?" He says, "I want to see thae boats." He really thought they brought out the boat from the Clyde up to the work to paint it!"

Thus the freedom of the 'privilege' apprenticeship was unusual, and the inflexibility of the system was revealed during the war when service with the forces disturbed the phasing of age and training. Peter Russell served in the Navy before he finished his time in Barr & Stroud's, and when released from the Navy carried on as before, but with a journeyman's wage:

'I had what they called an interrupted apprenticeship. I started my apprenticeship and I did two years of apprenticeship, right. And I got called up for the forces, I got called up for the Navy and I came back and the agreement was that I would continue my apprenticeship and finish my apprenticeship. And the government paid part of my wages and the firm paid my wages, you know, because they were still having to pay me a journeyman's rate, although officially I was still learning as an apprentice.'

In normal times, when national emergency did not provide a government subsidy, it was difficult to get training at any other than the traditional age, even if the delay was due to illness. Andrew Stuart, later a Lecturer in Springburn College, was fortunate, but his good luck was unusual:

'So, I was partially recovered, I could only take a light job, you know. I was seventeen by this time. There was a wee place in Annbank St, a tinsmith shop and I went there to start an apprenticeship, although I was a year late. Now that firm, after about two years or so it went flat and I was the only apprentice. No-one would accept me. I was too old, too old at eighteen you see. No, nineteen, because most of the apprenticeships stopped at twenty-one. No way could I do the five years in that time, you see. So, all this time I was studying, and a heating and ventilating firm took over the firm and me as an apprentice, and I finished my apprenticeship there.'

Sometimes an apprentice could not be guaranteed his whole apprenticeship time to be spent within one firm, and would have to look for another firm to let him complete his time. Joseph Docherty, a fitter in the Caley, underlines the importance for himself and his future career plans of not having an interrupted apprenticeship:

'Before I left the Caley I'd done about four years in the Caley and I finished my time when I came out. I finished it in a place where my brother worked, A & P Stevens. Used to be lift engineers. I done my last year in there. I could've been alright, I could have got credited with the time out of the army, but I preferred to have a complete set of papers. So I had four years of the railway, and a year of A & P Stevens to finish my time. So they're full apprenticeship papers, not counting the army.'

Even outside industry, apprenticeships were once an accepted and unquestioned part of working life, even if their traditions lived on by another name. Springburn was once the major shopping centre for the north of Glasgow, and Hoey's one of its chief retailers. The now familiar criticisms of perpetuated conservative trade practices, low pay and not being trained in the workplace but through night-classes, are just as apparent here as anywhere else. However, Hoey's did attempt to change with the times. Samuel Hoey is the grandson of the firm's founder, and his own time in training could be reasonably compared with a 'privileged' apprenticeship:

'I came into the business just as the war started. I'd been with

Copeland & Lyle and served my apprenticeship there, and then so many people were called up for the Services and I went into the business at that time but only for about a year, and I went away myself for five and a half years—I was in the RAF. Then I came back after that and took over at the China Department, hardware and china, because that's what I'd trained in basically. I'd trained in quite a number of other departments at Copeland & Lyle; I used to be down in the famous basement, the ironmongery basement at Copeland & Lyle which was well known. It was quite an interesting time of your life that, when as I say, there were about six or seven of us, all young boys who were possible managing directors of companies in years to come and many of the older people at Copeland & Lyle took great delight in kicking our behinds while they had the chance—if they didn't get in then, they'd never do it again, sort of thing! But it was a very good training indeed, an excellent training and they moved us from department to department of course, and gave us an idea of what was going on.'

Any special training given to the other staff was a reward for both diligence and ambition:

'We didn't have signed indentures in this sort of work, and really in those days that was quite rare. But my father might have had an indenture—he might have had to sign an indenture in those days. Probably not, for they had begun to die out. It was a proper gentleman's agreement that they would be paid a pittance! I did very well: I got 7/6 a week, but they would be paid a pittance usually to learn the trade. We had trained window dressers, yes, but almost all of us went to night-school to take classes. The College of Commerce was very often the place and we had four or five people who had taken courses, taken classes in window dressing. I used to do a lot of it myself at one time.

'The idea of training window dressers came up in my time, yes. I think the others more or less learned by the old training method. You know, "Sit next to Nellie," and you learned from what somebody else had done. Of course, that meant that you had a tradition that went on for years and years. The window had been dressed like that for twenty years and would continue to be dressed like that. We sent juniors to the College of Commerce to learn, sometimes window-dressing, sometimes ironmongery if it was to specialise there. There were special ironmongery classes, of course ... I mean it's incredible, you know, if you start looking at how many different kinds of window latch or how many different kinds of screws there are. We didn't stock full ranges or anything like that, but the trained ironmongers were expected to know the names of everything; trade names for tools, trade names for all kinds of things. I was never fully trained in that but I had a fair knowledge of them, but there are still things that I see and say, "What on earth was that?", you know, you have no idea what it was. Well, as

I say, we trained corsetieres who went down south to Berlei, to be trained there. That sort of thing, you know. We'd train fitters of course, for our Men's department and this kind of thing. We had a bit of training went on generally and that would be paid for by the firm. They would go to night-classes in their own time, of course, but eventually we began to let them off in the middle of the day to do things. But that was very much a new development and there'd only be certain people that would get to do that.'

When, in 1946, the NBL finally began manufacturing diesel engines, Springburn first encountered the problem of retraining on a major scale. German engineers were brought over to show the local men how to manufacture the Voith transmission for the MAN Diesel Hydraulic engines. The engines they made never met performance requirements and the Chairman, Coughtrie, blamed this on the workforce, saying that they were 'too steam-minded'. But this charge could equally have been made against management, who had, like the shopfloor workers, grown up with steam technology. Nor was abuse of the workers a substitute for a coherent retraining programme. While it is arguable that NBL wouldn't have survived anyway, the transfer to diesel, which was its only hope, was severely hampered by the tradition of learning on the job and of an artificially prolonged training period.

With nationalisation of the railways in 1948, including the Cowlairs and St Rollox Works, the new British Rail organisation was concerned to improve efficiency and to learn from Germany. Jimmy Robertson, a foreman in Cowlairs works, benefited from the new freedom on the continent. The clearest point of contrast with Britain is in the location of the training itself. In the German system, apprentices still did some of the work of the factory but in a separate place, isolated from the chaotic and unplanned nature of much of the apprentices' work on the factory floor in this country. The Germans combined both commercial utility and training simultaneously:

'I was sent to Germany on an exchange visit to the German railways. We were there for a fortnight, twelve of us from all over Britain. I was the only one from here. In Germany, the training school was away from the works altogether. The apprentices were in the training school for the whole of their apprenticeship, you see, but they did productive work. Certain jobs, instead of sending them to the works, they sent them to the training school. Now, when you finished your time, when you went into the training school, you got a go at everything: machines, turning, coachbuilding, you name it, you had a go. They had a five-year apprenticeship, but they were never in the works. But the training school was a works just the same, and they did productive work, they weren't just playing about with toys, or anything like that, they were actually making something. At the end of your apprenticeship, they decided what you were best at, you understand, and they sent you to be a coachbuilder, a wagonbuilder; you were a railway shopman. They've now got that title in British railways. So that was how they did it in Germany.' Again however, even if the lessons were well learned, external events were the decisive factors: the competition from the new motorways and the policy of centralisation in the south led to the closure of the Cowlairs Works in 1968 and reduction of St Rollox to a maintenance depot in 1986–7.

The apprenticeship system was an important defence of the original trade unions, protecting wages by restricting entry to trades. One of its consequences was the division of the labour force into two quite distinct groups: 'skilled' and 'unskilled', which in turn became the major social division within the working class. The apprenticeship system also suited employers as it provided a pool of skilled labour to choose from, so that skilled workers never became scarce enough for wages to rise beyond an employer's control. This same labour force was then continually renewed by training which was done at the point of manufacture, and paid for by wages that were artificially restrained by reference to an apprentice's age.

With the spread of the industrial revolution throughout Europe, Britain lost its place as 'workshop of the world', and increasingly found her markets threatened from abroad. Fearing this competition, employers began to introduce methods of production that would increase efficiency. In engineering, this almost invariably meant more machine-based work. Machine-work, it was thought, would not only increase productivity, but also effectively de-skill labour, and thus enable wages to be reduced. There was smaller scope for individual craft practices on a machine designed for mass manufacture. However though these new processes did reduce the amount of skill required for many jobs, apprenticeship as a tradition was virtually unaffected by the increased mechanisation and carried on, almost unchanged, into the twentieth century. In some cases its status was strengthened—any employer who succeeded in breaking down a manufacturing process to its consituent parts would have actually increased specialisation in no small measure. The skills learned by apprentices became less and less transferable, and more and more restricted to a particular workshop.

In the *Economic Journal* in 1909, RH Tawney wrote a powerful essay, critical of the apprenticeship system, based on an analysis of a number of firms, including the North British Locomotive Company. Before the school-leaving age was raised, boys had a two-year gap between leaving school and being eligible for an apprenticeship. This meant two years of casual work, and the acquisition of bad habits that were a poor preparation for a disciplined working life. The subsequent five-year apprenticeship was too long and encouraged laziness in both journeyman and apprentice. Young men then quickly became disillusioned with the training they received, and many went back to casual or labouring work, where the immediate rewards were higher.

Apart from the psychological cost to the individual, and the social cost to the community in disappointing the best expectations of its youngest adults, Tawney's chief criticism is an economic one. He felt that training as specialised as an apprentice's meant little or no adaptability to the jobs market. The instability of commercial life meant that apprenticeships were an act of unnecessary and costly confinement. By restricting themselves to one limited trade, young men painted themselves into a corner which the economy of the country could ill afford. If the economy was to modernise properly, then it would need an adaptable workforce. This adaptability required 'general industrial knowledge and intelligence' as its main elements, something that apprenticeships conspicuously failed to provide.

Tawney's thesis shows remarkable prescience at a time when the underlying problems in the economy were not widely appreciated. In 1905, NBL reached a level of production which it never achieved again, and a greater tonnage was shifted on the Clyde in 1913 than at any time before or since. Thus he wrote at the time of Scottish engineering's peak, when it appeared unimaginable that it would not always lead the world. His criticisms remain valid and are borne out by interviews conducted almost three generations later. Apprenticeships were just one aspect of an increasingly anachronistic system; their survival prolonged by the entanglement with attempts to improve productivity. Still, it would be difficult to underestimate the problems of transforming a process that had over a number of generations become part of the way of life of the entire country. Apprenticeship was seen not only to reward intelligence and diligence but also to underpin community values such as deference, thrift and patience.

The decline of heavy industry, with its large employers and craft tradition, brought the decline of apprenticeship. Access to skilled work now requires a higher academic achievement than the old system and the range of jobs open to people is much wider. Today, training is available in a great variety of ways, including day release, full-time in colleges of further education or specialised colleges. The object is the replacement of the old system by one which provides both flexible and high quality training to meet the needs of industry. There is still a skills shortage however and it is arguable that not enough has been done to re-educate people who were brought up in a culture where training was based on apprenticeship, so that they can use the new opportunities to the full. The new Employment Training scheme amalgamates over thirty separate training programmes and places much greater emphasis on job related training. It is being implemented at the time of writing and it is too early to assess its success.

Andrew 'Punch' MacMillan as an apprentice blacksmith in Hyde Park. Skills were passed from one generation to the next through the apprenticeship system.

Jimmy Vaughan as an office boy in 1923. He began his apprenticeship in the carriage shop in 1925 and retired in 1972, having spent his entire working life in the 'Caley'.

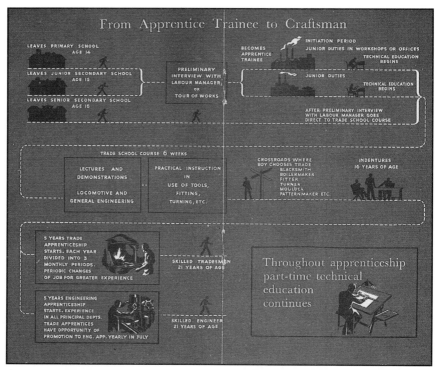

From Apprentice Trainee to Craftsman

LEAVES PRIMARY SCHOOL
AGE 14

LEAVES JUNIOR SECONDARY SCHOOL
AGE 15

LEAVES SENIOR SECONDARY SCHOOL
AGE 16

PRELIMINARY INTERVIEW WITH LABOUR MANAGER, or TOUR OF WORKS

BECOMES APPRENTICE TRAINEE

INITIATION PERIOD
JUNIOR DUTIES IN WORKSHOPS OR OFFICES
TECHNICAL EDUCATION BEGINS

JUNIOR DUTIES
TECHNICAL EDUCATION BEGINS

AFTER PRELIMINARY INTERVIEW WITH LABOUR MANAGER GOES DIRECT TO TRADE SCHOOL COURSE

TRADE SCHOOL COURSE 6 WEEKS

LECTURES AND DEMONSTRATIONS

LOCOMOTIVE AND GENERAL ENGINEERING

PRACTICAL INSTRUCTION IN USE OF TOOLS, FITTING, TURNING, ETC.

CROSSROADS WHERE BOY CHOOSES TRADE
BLACKSMITH
BOILERMAKER
FITTER
TURNER
MOULDER
PATTERNMAKER ETC.

INDENTURES
16 YEARS OF AGE

5 YEARS TRADE APPRENTICESHIP STARTS. EACH YEAR DIVIDED INTO 3 MONTHLY PERIODS. PERIODIC CHANGES OF JOB FOR GREATER EXPERIENCE

SKILLED TRADESMEN
21 YEARS OF AGE

5 YEARS ENGINEERING APPRENTICESHIP STARTS. EXPERIENCE IN ALL PRINCIPAL DEPTS. TRADE APPRENTICES HAVE OPPORTUNITY OF PROMOTION TO ENG. APP. YEARLY IN JULY

SKILLED ENGINEER
21 YEARS OF AGE

Throughout apprenticeship part-time technical education continues

A page from a North British Locomotive Company recruitment booklet, showing the predictable course of a career based on apprenticeship.

Ian Laval, sheet metal gold medallist at the Sixteenth International Apprentices Competition in Madrid in 1967. Mr Laval trained in Springburn College of Engineering, formerly the headquarters of the North British Locomotive Company. Mr Laval's award reflected not only his individual talent and those of his teacher Andrew Stuart, but the tradition of high skill which survived in the area for some time after the works closed.

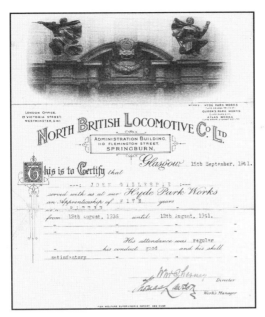

Apprenticeship Certificate presented to John Gillespie by the North British Locomotive Company in 1941. The design on the top of the certificate is from over the door of NBL's office building (1909), which survives today as Springburn College.

Apprenticeship Certificate presented to Thomas Stewart by Neilson and Co in 1894.

4

HEALTH
& SAFETY

HEALTH AND SAFETY

Of all the possible areas of a working life where parliamentary attention has been focussed, perhaps the Industrial Health and Safety regulations betray most clearly the slow and piecemeal pattern of uninformed legislation, and its limitations. The halting pace of the first reforms can be partly explained by the fact that the people who suffered most from poor working conditions were simply not represented in Parliament. This would also explain the tone of this first protective legislation of the modern industrial age, which sought to marry concern for the individual's welfare with the upkeep of his moral character, as for example in the Health and Morals of Apprentices Act of 1802.

Until the last two decades of the nineteenth century, politicians reacted only to certain 'exposed' evils affecting the new working classes. By that time, the later Reform Acts had enfranchised a wider section of the public and made possible a wider appreciation of the problems of unsafe and unhealthy working conditions. Nevertheless, right up to the middle of the twentieth century, what truly marks parliamentary concern about working conditions is not the inadequacy of its legislation, but the insincerity of its vigilance. At the turn of the century, there were a total of 113 Factory Inspectors expected to supervise nearly 250 000 factories and workshops. Just more than fifty years later, and although the Factory Inspectorate was better staffed and more professional than ever before, the pressure of work was still too great.

Mr McLean is now the head of the Health and Safety Executive for the West of Scotland, but was previously the Factory Inspector for Glasgow Central & District in the late 1950s, an area which included Springburn. At that time, a Factory Inspector's workload was divided geographically, and not by industry as it is at present. Glasgow Central was an area that took in Glasgow north of the river from Anderston eastwards, and included north-east Glasgow, Argyllshire and the outer islands. The staff covering this area would consist of one District Inspector in charge, and he or she would have at most two fully-trained Inspectors and a trainee to assist them. This was obviously inadequate, and it is testimony to the Inspectorate's tenacity that such infrequent visitors are so clearly remembered:

'At that time we were still responsible for a lot of very small premises, because we would have registered on our books, for example, practically every butchers' shop, because in Glasgow every butchers' shop manufactured its own sausages. Every little bake-house that did a little bit of baking on the premises would be registered for the manufacture of confectionery and baking, so that in a place like Springburn, where you would have a shopping centre, you would have quite a lot of work just looking at the very small places that are now done by the local authorities. You look at the butchers' shops, you look at the mincing machines, the sausage-linking machines and things like that. You'd look at all sorts of toilet accommodation, their general cleanliness, the way they went about themselves generally. You'd be looking at dry-cleaning establishments, because dry-cleaning establishments normally had their press at the back. You'd have cobblers' shops where you were doing shoe-repairing, again with a certain amount of machinery, a certain amount of dust problems. You'd a whole range of little places, little joiners' shops where they would be preparing work for the joiners to do on-site. The pattern of trade, of course, has changed quite a lot. I mean, a lot of the small bake-houses have disappeared, because people buy their stuff from supermarkets, and you get the in-store baker in the supermarket, which would now be inspected by a local authority inspector, not the Factory Inspector.'

These facts demonstrate the limitations of the Factory Inspectorate, but this is not to underestimate their importance. The larger engineering works, or at least the shop-floor management, including those in Springburn's railway works, would always make some attempt to apply the legislation. In doing so, they responded positively to the Factory Inspectors' first priority, the encouragement of self-regulation. For the Factory Inspectorate this was, of course, making a virtue out of necessity. But the engineering companies could not afford many run-ins with a regulatory authority. It would be bad for their reputations, bad for shopfloor relations and bad for completion of orders.

Records of railway accidents were made by Board of Trade Inspectors from the late 1840s, and covered accidents in the works when the movement of a locomotive, carriage or wagon was involved. The following is a typical example:

'Inquiry into an accident that occurred on the 5th October, 1908, to engine shed labourer Alexander Walkinshaw at St Rollox.

'At 12.30 p.m, Walkinshaw was engaged in removing some broken bricks which, on being taken from an engine fire-box, had been placed in the six-foot space between No. 2 and No. 3 lines outside the shed.

'Walkinshaw had previously set his wheel-barrow in a safe position between the two lines mentioned, but whilst walking through the yard engine driver A. McMinn seeing an engine running on No. 2 line and not knowing that Walkinshaw had been warned of the movement, called to Walkinshaw to "mind" his barrow, on which, although the engine had then partly passed in safety, Walkinshaw attempted to move the barrow, and in doing so he pushed it foul, with the result that the barrow was struck by an axlebox of the tender and he was knocked down, sustaining injury to his chest and left leg.

'Walkinshaw is 69 years of age. His regular working hours are $11\frac{1}{2}$, and at the time of the mishap he had been on duty $6\frac{1}{2}$ hours.

'In this case I think the accident should be attributed to misadventure.'

This extract makes clear a number of points. Old age pensions had been introduced in 1907, but only for people over seventy, so that men either had to work until that age, be completely dependent on their families if they had one, or look for Poor Relief. Though recording his age, the report does not record his physical condition after a lifetime of labouring. It also makes clear that the railway company was not responsible for the safety of workers unless the company itself could be shown to be at fault.

Records of accidents also appeared in a local newspaper published independently by a Springburn man called George Hutchison between 1893 and 1908 in Springburn Road. The *St Rollox and Springburn Express* covered events in an area from Townhead, through Springburn and Possil to the beginnings of what later became Milton. A weekly paper, it was unashamedly local in content, but the accidents usually received no more than a cursory mention. It is quite revealing to list a few. To take a short period in 1899, a not untypical series of reports are:

"March 9th—Caledonian Railway Works. Man crushed by wagons. Dies in Royal Infirmary."

"March 9th—Springburn Goods station. Engine driver falls onto rails and fractures left leg."

"March 16th—Cowlairs Works. Man's trousers caught by revolving wheel. Severe lacerations above right knee."

"March 16—Clydesdale Iron Works. Man struck on chest by hammer. Dies fortnight later."

"May 11th—Hyde Park railway works. Man drilling steel plate which overturned and fell on top of him. Severe internal injuries."

Even the non-fatal injuries are all severe and disabling. Most injuries concern accidentally dropping weights or someone just falling over, or some other accident that shows that a person was less than completely aware of what was going on around them. This bespoke a fatigue brought on not just by the working conditions and the nature of the work itself, but by lengthy working hours. By the beginning of the First World War, it was still the practice for people to work five ten-hour days and a sixth six-and-a-half hour day in the average working week. Even these hours, though, were the result of repeated challenges to accepted working practices. In 1890, there was a concerted railway strike by guards, firemen, signalmen, and drivers, many from Springburn. They were fighting for the instatement of a ten-hour maximum day and the recognition of their union. Their hours until that point had been a 144-hour fortnight, involving not the expected 12-hour shifts, but much longer shifts dependent entirely on train schedules. Overtime was compulsory and could lead to shifts of more than twenty hours or more on consecutive days. In December 1891, 275, or 82.34%, of the Caledonian Railway's 334 passenger drivers and firemen worked more than twelve hours a day on 1331 occasions. In other words, most drivers worked more than twelve hours nearly five times that month, without a rest of eight hours before their next shift. (Board of Trade, cd6796, 1892, p. 62) The strike was defeated in 1891 with no concessions granted, with the result that the number of railway accidents caused by exhausted workers rose sharply in the 1890s. At the end of World War I, the working week in general was reduced to 48 hours a week, and that remained the norm for the next 40 years.

People who remember a more recent past still have important contributions to make to our understanding of the progress made in the last two generations. Their response to any questions on this matter was immediately and compulsively anecdotal; their opinions are shaped primarily by their own experiences.

Although later a draughtsman with the North British Locomotive Company, Willie Dewar began his working life as a message-boy and used to travel the length and breadth of the works. He got to know all the working practices and their limitations very well. He demonstrates just how indifferent many people were to their particular working environment. This could be the result of working for the same company for a whole lifetime, but it is more likely to be that dangers and unpleasantness were simply accepted as part and parcel of a working life. This is made plain by what he describes as 'minor' accidents:

'The furnace men were protected with bags round their heads, like those wee hoods which came down the side, and something down their arms, and bags down their legs—probably something like moleskin bags. The brickies used to wear covers like hoods when they went into the boilers to do the work, for the boiler was still hot... We didn't wear glasses to protect our eyes. In fact, in the Atlas Works, they had a cylinder boring machine there at one time, and the wee labourer that did all the work cleaning the table of the machine, his skin was polished actually—the cast iron dust was ingrained into his skin. I don't know whether he washed properly when he went home, but this is how he was. Now that man probably died with something in the lungs for all we know: it was just wee Jimmy from the railway. "Look, he's covered in cast iron!", and that was a laugh, you know, nobody bothered. It was the same with protection in guillotines. It was only when the Factory Inspectors came in to complain that we had to do something with the guards. But the men didn't want to use the guards, because it was restricting them. They didn't have the hydraulic systems

G

that they have now, where the machines won't operate unless the guard is down... What I drew once—it was to satisfy the Factory Inspector —was to make a wire guard which he put down before he actually worked the machine. But it was in his road, so, if you went down the shop, the guard was tied up.

'I would say a big number of eye accidents could probably have been prevented, for instance me getting a fire in my eye when I was working in that Klondyke Department. If I'd had these protection glasses on, that wouldn't have happened... It was a common thing that you went to the ambulance man with something in your eye, and if he couldn't get it out, he gave you a token and a bit of cotton wool, and you went down to the Eye Infirmary. It was a well-kitted out ambulance room: they had everything in it.'

Andy Stuart, a fitter and subsequently a foreman in Metropolitan Vickers confirms these memories:

'Guards on machines would all have notices, DO NOT REMOVE, but workmen would remove the guards for better access. Foremen and chargehands would also ignore the removal, but senior management wouldn't, and often would read the "Riot Act" to all offenders, resulting occasionally in suspensions and dismissals.'

'When a welder first strikes the workpiece with the electrode, anyone nearby could get a flash in their eyes, if the welder's work is not surrounded by screens. Usually the pain occurs much later (very often through the night) and the eyes water greatly and feel as if they have sand in them. Relief could only be got if the Eye Infirmary attends to it. Strange to say, if the victim went to the Royal or Stobhill Emergencies, their inexperience with such injuries caused even more pain.'

The quality of the relationship with management, and foremen in particular, was an important factor in assessing the working environment. Bob Kenny worked in Hyde Park before taking a chance to leave for better working conditions (even at the cost of a drop in wages) in the Craigpark Cable Company. He shows how petty feuding and interference could spoil a shopfloor relationship. Hyde Park was an old-fashioned works both in terms of safety regulations and of working conditions. It was primitive by modern standards, even by the standards of the time, when compared with more enlightened employers such as Craigpark. As usual, eye injuries predominated; the road from any engineering works in Glasgow to the Eye Infirmary in Sauchiehall Street must have been a well-worn one:

'The foreman would come through the work at a particular time— this was the nightshift. You would hear the door clanging, and you knew that was him on his way, so everybody's at their machine, and he walked up and then he walked back, and as soon as he was away the cans came out. They made their tea in cans... But this time the door clanged, and of course they're expecting him to come in, but he didn't come in, so they waited, then eventually they went and got their cans. And of course he had just waited until he knew that they were set up. Then he walked up the shop this time. Of course they couldn't go, and what he did was he went up to the fire with all the cans and just stood and waited until the behind burnt out of the cans and then he just walked away again. It was a sort of unofficial tea break.

'In general, it was pretty cold in Hyde Park. The roofs were really high, you know, they had great big four foot ducting that went right along the place for heating, which didn't really heat the place. They had these big char fires and I can remember, the drill was, you had a certain amount of work to do. You hammered in as hard as you could to get it done and it gave you a break, about fifteen minutes or something. You went to this char fire to stand round the fires, and we came to a place which was locked, and it was always locked. The likes of myself, younger, used to ask the older men, what was this place. "Oh, I don't know really what's in it. It's a wash place or something." Eventually they got it opened and it was lined with wash basins, and we said "How is it never used? How is it locked?." Well, apparently the thing was that when they were looking into the conditions of the workers and that, there was a decree made that they had to have washhand basins, and they put in washhand basins, but they didn't go to the expense of putting water in... They went as far as the law was asking them to go.

'You got any kind of safety equipment you needed. Eyes was the most protected, especially if you were on the brass—it broke into small parts and flew up... But you got caught an odd time, and you'd go to the Eye Infirmary and get something removed from your eye. But once you had had that once, you didn't get caught again, you wore whatever protection you needed. The stuff was supplied—goggles and gloves and things like that.'

John Wotherspoon worked in St Rollox and witnessed many accidents:

'I've seen a man being killed in the works. He was what they called the lookout man. When the stock was being brought into the works they had to close the doors to keep the heat in. So when they were bringing carriages into the shop the doors were thrown open and there was a man at the door to see everyone was kept out of danger. Well, after the shunt had been brought in, this old bloke, he comes in for a heat in the shop, and, unknown to him they had brought a shunt in, and it comes right through the door. He was standing at the back of the door and he was killed. He was the look out man too... I've seen one of the shunters killed, but I saw other accidents that were pretty serious accidents.'

As a shop steward, Mr Wotherspoon was very concerned to improve safety standards and had to struggle both in educating both work-force and in negotiating with management to see the sense in prevention:

'It was a big part of your duties, to see to the safety. It was a thing we had forced on the companies. The companies were duty bound by the Board of Trade rules to do this and to do that and the next thing, but as long as they stuck up that notice, that was all the responsibility they accepted. You had to speak to men and stop them doing certain operations because they were endangering themselves by carrying out shortcuts and using tools they shouldn't be using—they were damaged in some way and you'd say "Better go back up to the foreman and get that hammer changed." I felt it was my responsibility to carry it out. Other delegates didn't. But the way I looked at it, I had been in courts too often, and we had lost too many cases, and so much blame in the courts put on the men, because he's a skilled worker, he's responsible. It's amazing how the company gets around this and they win their case. Well, I says the place to win their cases is in the workshop: stop it before it happens. And I used to fall out with many a man. I'd say "Look, stop doing that, for goodness sake, you know what happened with so and so the last time."'

Belonging to a different generation, when much higher standards of health and safety were taken for granted, Ian Rankin began his apprenticeship as a painter in the St Rollox Works in 1979. The emphasis on personal responsibility for safety is clear from his account:

'You got overalls or 'Ovies', and a jacket. My overalls were bogging. I could never keep them clean, keep the paint off them, used to take them off and they would just stand up by themselves—I was the worst: everybody else had nice clean overalls and I'm walking about with stiff legs. You got rubber gloves issued to you for doing all the mucky jobs. The "Toetectors" van would come into the works, and you would buy them (boots) off the van and that would get paid up every week. It would get taken off your wages. Hard hats were available, but you had to ask for them: nobody told you hard hats were available. When we were doing the spray polishing on these big panels for the inside of the coaches, we got issued with respirators, like wee Biggles masks. They figured that the fumes off the paint we were using weren't dangerous. See, it was enamel paints we used and they were mostly lead free. But you're working on a big area and there were extractors, so all the fumes went away. The only times you ever got the fumes was if you were in the cab of a driving coach, you know the diesel multiple unit, if you were in the cab of one of them, or in the guard's dookit.'

Clearly these represent a great improvement on the standards of forty years earlier. Mr Rankin's subsequent experience with a car hire firm illustrates that, compared to the railway industry, the demands of commercial enterprise are likely to marginalise these matters:

'There wasn't any working conditions. There was just this big concrete floor. There was a dry bit at one end and wet bit at the other. You got a pair of wellies, but they never fitted. I think they bought a job lot of wellies from a person with enormously large feet, so they wouldn't fit anybody, and everybody would be in the same boat, or wellie... You had a wee bothy to sit in, but you didn't have a locker or anything. The dry bit was where you checked the oil and water in the motors, the wet bits where you washed them. Used to get absolutely soaked. I hated it. At dinner time you'd be walking about the town wringing wet, bogging, stinking, you know. Washing facilities were virtually non-existent, a wee sink in the toilet which you could use.'

Joe Amato worked in Braby's, in the galvanising section, starting before the war, and met his wife, Alice, there during the war, when she was directed there for war-work. He demonstrates just how much could be taken for granted in a workplace before awareness of safety or health matters became of primary importance,

'I don't recall a bad accident, and I was in it for thirty years. You might get someone hitting their thumb with a hammer... It wasn't what I would say a tough department, [galvanising], but it was a very unhealthy department. You used to have to use an awful lot of saltpetre when they were dipping the tank and that metal, and they used to throw handfuls of that saltpetre to help clean it, and it gave off powerful fumes. Never seen anybody wearing a mask. It wasn't compulsory, but now it would be compulsory. Just as now it's compulsory to wear ear-muffs. All you used to do was take a lump of cotton wool and stick it in your ear.'

Craigpark Cables was always a good place to work in Springburn, and this is borne out by Mr Morrison, for whom the one serious accident stands out because of its rarity:

'I can only remember one serious accident. There's a large laying-up machine, it was about twenty feet high, it's a grey rotating thing. These big drums of these cores were put in these cradles and the whole thing rotated and laid up the cable. There was a fellow, he must have fallen into this machine as these great drums went round, he must have slipped. Anyway, he slipped in. Fortunately the machine was coming away from this concrete pit that it was installed in. If it had been going the other way it would have wiped him against the concrete, and it took him up in the air, and by the time one of the other chaps could get to the thing and press the button, it had gone over the top and it threw him out over the other side. He'd ever so many broken bones, and was off for months, but later, he was a good chap, he came to Scottish Cables, the firm I was with later...'

Women's work often involved using skills similar to those involved in managing a home, especially cleaning and caring for others. The low value placed on women's labour was reflected in the wages they received. Cleaners received what was known as a 'secondary', or supplementary wage. It was assumed that the family would be supported in the main by a father's or a husband's wages. Thus even if the work was as hard as that of men, the wages were substantially less. Men did not have a monopoly of physical exertion and decades of demanding repetitive activities could undoubtedly cause damage to a person's well-being. Agnes Muirhead was a cleaner, and she reveals the dangers inherent but so often undetected in so-called 'menial' work:

'There was no electric machinery or anything like that; it was all down on your knees scrubbing. For polishing, you used what they termed a buffing block, a 'jock'. We called it a jock. It had a long handle, a swivel handle, it was a block about two foot by one foot, but it was heavy weighted, and you put a flannel underneath the block. So you swung it, and you rubbed the polish into the floor, and you swung this jock, backwards and forwards. Now I've been in contact with quite a few that worked with me in these years, and I would say that nine out of ten complained of having a fallen womb. So they blamed the jock for it. Whether that had anything to do with it, I don't know. But nine out of ten, it seemed to affect them.'

Mrs Muirhead always worked outside the home, and her experience is fairly typical. For many women however, their first or only experience of paid work or of factory work took place during the war years. This makes their experiences more distinct and, being unique in their working life, more memorable. Mary Williamson worked in Hyde Park works during the war, and she shows that the slightest lapse from the rules, usually involving a shortcut, could easily lead to an accident,

'One girl was working a turning machine and her hair got caught, and her face was battered, you know. And there was another wee girl from Auchinairn, she was pulled into a machine, but one of the men was quick to put off the machine. I had one myself, but I'd only six stitches in my hand. One of the men was working late that night, and he came round and asked me to bore something. When we were boring we always set up a stopper, and he says, "I don't think you'll need the stopper for this, Mary," so I just held it, pulled down my drill and it jumped off the machine. I had to get six stitches in my hand... You always had guards on your machines. Well, I hadn't a guard on my machine, it was only a tiny wee machine I worked, because I was just classed as an apprentice. But we always had stoppers and clamps to clamp all your jobs down before you could use your drill on them, you know, just so happened that night I didn't clamp anything down.' By this time most machines had their own power source, whereas a generation before Mrs Williamson arrived in Hyde Park, overhead shafting was the normal state of affairs. The Factory Inspector, Mr McLean, attested that the end of overhead cabling was one of the most positive aspects of twentieth century factory life. (A more detailed account of women's wartime work is given in a separate chapter.)

Before World War II, the main preoccupation of workers and trades unions was wages rather than working conditions—the risks were accepted as an unavoidable part of the job, at a time when high unemployment reduced workers' bargaining power. The vast improvement in health and safety which has been made, especially since the end of the Second World War, is one of the greatest achievements of the labour movement. The horrific conditions endured in the relatively recent past now seem remote, showing how quickly such hard-won improvements are taken for granted.

A Cowlairs first aid team posing for their former colleague William Graham. He had not been re-employed after the 1890/91 Strike, and turned his hobby of photography into a profession.

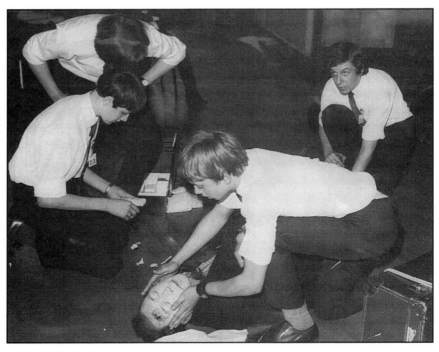

A first aid team from the Glasgow (St Rollox) Works at a competition in Derby in 1970. The apprentices were (top left) W Armour, (left) E McLoin, (top right) G Combes and M Breen. They came fourth out of thirteen teams.

Toilets in the St Rollox Works before the modernisation of 1964-68. These urinals were used by 299 men.

Willie Dewar supervising the loading of a YP Class 4-8-0 locomotive on board ship at Finnieston. This was one of an order of a hundred engines built for India in 1951-2.

The Marne Flanging Shop in the Atlas Works, 1930. Men removing the steel plate from the furnace.

Removing the completed flanged plate from the hydraulic press.

Willie Dewar remembers the flanging process from the 1940s. 'The men wore only bags as protection against the heat, and they lifted the great big plates with a thing like a big fork, suspended in the middle from the crane, and about half a dozen men got on to the outside of it—it was pivoted. You could put the fork in below the plates, big open arm thing, and the men leant on this—the weight of them could lift it, it was in balance. And the furnacemen opened the door about six inches, and the men were protected with bags.'

The galvanising and pickling shop at Braby's Eclipse works about 1900.

St Rollox machine shop about 1900, when dangerous overhead shafting was still the norm.

St Rollox machine and brass shop about 1968.

Alford Street Branch of the Cowlairs Cooperative Society in the early 1950s.

5

WARWORK & WOMEN

WAR WORK AND WOMEN

Springburn's great heavy engineering resources were called into service in both World Wars. Most of its skilled workers were in reserved occupations, deemed to be crucial to production of war material. The scale of its capacity, energy and achievement can be gauged from the contribution made by the North British Locomotive Company to the 1914–18 war. The main works continued to produce locomotives, of which 1412 were built between 1914 and 1918. Of these, 695 were produced for use in the war area, about 380 going to France and 300 being built for the Ministry of Munitions for overseas service. In addition they produced aeroplanes (BE 2C's), torpedo tubes, Medium and Mark VIII tanks, 18 pounder gun carriages and machine tools for other works. Two buildings which were in the course of construction when war broke out were named the Mons and the Marne after early battles. During the course of the war the Mons produced 864 551 shells and the Marne produced 477 438 forgings and 6000 sea mines. They also produced pill-boxes and machine gun casemates. This work was mainly carried out by women, of whom 1781 were employed during the war, as 3120 of NBL's 1914 employees enlisted in the armed forces. In spite of the rapid induction of an untrained workforce and the strain and fatigue caused by long hours of heavy work, the NBL was able to boast that there were no fatal injuries in the works during 1914–19.

In the Second World War, Springburn's works were also devoted to war production, again supplying both locomotives and munitions on a vast scale. John Menzies remembers working in St Rollox at this time:

'This was in the critical period of the war. We were working twelve hour shifts, 6 am to 6 pm, and that applied to everyone. Some shops, notably the machine shop, the Brass shop and part of the erecting shop, worked double shifts, that was alternate dayshift and nightshift, 6 am to 6 pm, 6 pm to 6 am. The dayshift also worked 6 am to 10 pm on Saturdays. We had two meal breaks, from 10 to 10.30 in the morning and 2 to 2.30 in the afternoon. The nightshift had corresponding ones during the night. We were somewhat in advance of the time, however, in that we had recognised breaks in addition for tea. We had trolleys which came round the works, dispensing tea and biscuits, I suppose it would be some wartime delicacy. I don't remember exactly what it was like, but these trolleys came round at fixed times. If I remember rightly, it was 8.30 in the morning and 4 o'clock in the afternoon. The idea behind this was to stop people going off and having unofficial breaks, and it worked very well. I don't think it was terribly widespread, but certain other firms did it and I did overhear, I remember clearly, a conversation on a tram one evening by two bowler hatted gentlemen, discussing what was going on in the various works around the city, mentioning the point about the tea trolleys, and saying that it was terrible how workmen had to be pampered these days. So, I suppose it was in some ways a reward for working the long hours.'

For men in the factories, war work was dissimilar in quantity, but not in kind, from their peacetime tasks. Perhaps the single most memorable aspect of war work for our interviewees, therefore, is the participation of a whole generation of women in heavy industry.

After World War I, women munitions workers, whether they wished to or not, had to give up their jobs to the returning soldiers in 1918. The exception were menial jobs like carriage cleaning, for which women could be paid less than men, without threatening craft wage levels. Thus, for the generation born during or just after the first war, the second was a novel, demanding and often exciting time of unprecedented economic independence. Women had worked in many types of industry, but the wars were the first occasions on which they were admitted to heavy engineering factories, traditionally an exclusively male preserve. Maisie Gordon, for one, was not however as impressed with the work done in the factories as she had expected to be:

'I was at the Hyde Park, in the machine shop, a slinger. It was good. You'd often say to yourself, when I saw a workman coming out of Hyde Park with a dirty face and dirty hands—when I was younger, to me that man grafted. You thought, you know, "Oh my God, that man's doing a lot of work," and you'd go into it and they're not grafting, you know, it's so comical. You know you say to yourself, "My God, I mind when thae men were like slaves," you know, when they were really hard done by.'

For some women, war work was not their first paid employment but a transfer from other types of work. Agnes Muirhead worked before her arrival in the works as a conductress on the Glasgow trams. She gives a real flavour of war-time panic in her account of a trip in her tram during the Clydebank blitz:

'I started in the trams, before I went into Hyde Park. I was two years in the trams. The first night we had an air-raid here, I was in the trams running from St Vincent Street to Saracen Cross, Saracen Cross to St Vincent Street, St Vincent Street—Lambhill—St Vincent Street— Springburn Terminus. That was the runs, you see, short runs. So we had been down St Vincent Street and of course this air-raid warning. So this Inspector jumped onto the bus, and behind him was one of these ARP wardens. He said "Didn't you hear the sirens?" I says I'm going to jump off at Saracen. But do you know that that driver went right out that Lambhill Road without stopping! And we could see the flames in the distance, and it was an ARP warden who came on just before we went into Lambhill, and it was me—funny how it was always the conductor—that got it. He jumped on and he says to me, "Are you off your head?'', I said ''No, ask the driver if he's off his head!'' I asked what's been bombed or set on fire, and he said, ''It's oil tanks round about Clydebank.'' '

Training for women before they entered the works could never hope to be as comprehensive and complete as a young man's apprenticeship, and an immediate talent for a certain type of work would lead to being assigned to that task for the duration of the war. Not only was time precious, but there were agreements with the unions involved that limited women to, at best, semi-skilled status. This does not however, in any way, reduce the skill involved, since there was such a compressed training schedule. Even the vocabulary that covered these detailed negotiations, concerning the 'dilution of labour', reveals the terms by which women were contracted in and out of certain workplaces. Places that had strong traditions of skilled labour, such as the railway works or the shipyards, were especially antipathetic to the introduction of women. Maisie Gordon remembers:

'The Marne was a part of Atlas, which was a flanging shop. We were in the flanging shop. Now we went to training school in Springburn: Cowlairs Road. I think it was a six weeks, eight weeks or something, it was something like that anyway, and you had to pass tests. I went in as an acetylene burner. I was sent to the NBL, but I was on the Marne side. Now there was only two of us; a Miss McCabe and myself. Two women, that's all, the rest was all men. It was three furnaces for the flanging of tender blocks and what-have-ye, for the engines for abroad. We were only there for the first week and there was no work for us, but they couldn't pay us off. So they asked if we'd like to try electric welding. So we were put into cubicles, they were like horse-boxes. So we were given scrap and an electric rod that was put in through a holder. You switched on the electric, it was like electric welding and it came up in sort of bubbles, then ye chipped the scale off the top and seen what like it was. If you held it too long, naturally it was a hole. We were at that for quite a wee while, and Mr Craig, the foremen, came down one day and he says to me, ''Right, wee one''—I was always the wee one because I was small compared to Cathy Craig—''We're bringing in an overhead acetylene burner, and you're going on it, now,'' he says. I had a habit of skipping, och, all over the shop. The men would say, ''How would ye like to try the flanging?'' Anything, yes, ye weren't handling anything, ye were only pulling a lever. And BANG! the presses BANG! were coming BANG! up, you know, BANG! and putting it into shape, and then you were releasing it, and the men were taking it off. But I was always skipping up and down the shop if there was no work. Anyroad, he says, ''When this machine comes in, you stay at that machine.'' So they brought in this overhead machine, and there was a template on it. Now you had risen off the floor about four feet, you had a square box, and across it was bars, and there was four big iron holders. Now a big plate came down, and maybe you'd put twelve angle-irons onto it. So they were put onto this square, and ye set your template overhead, ye set it to that, so that you could cut so many out of that, then when that one was finished...''

Mary Smith was employed to do unskilled but very heavy work, including lifting fifty six pound shells, when the shortage of men became acute:

'I started in Hyde Park in October 1941. And at that time there was really no vacancies—they said that there wasn't a job in the Atlas Works that couldn't be done by a woman, except to load the shells. Now we didn't work actually in the place, we worked where the loading trucks came in from the railway line, you see. So, I was only nineteen at the time. The rest came from Possil, from Bishopbriggs and they were used to hard work because they used to work in the fields, you know, lifting potatoes, lifting turnips, working in the brickwork. They were used to heavy work. However it was a very, very happy crowd, it really was. In between loading, see, these shells had to be painted with a yellow flat paint and they used to have what they called a grommet, which was an oiled rope that would go round the copper band. So these were painted and then they were grommeted. They weighed fifty-six pounds each. There were ten to a load and it was an old rickety barrow with two shafts straight up, not even a bar, two long shafts. It took two of us to push it because it had big iron wheels, the iron would be about two inches wide you know. And ten was a lot, so we had to wait—it had to be teeped. This girl did nothing else but she had a wee hammer and she had three or four inches long pieces of metal, and that kept the lot number, so we knew exactly what lot to shift. And that was taken over a railway line and packed into the railway wagons. So to get up to the wagons we had to stand in a barrow ... a huge thing with big, big wheels, heavy and anchored with a couple of bricks. And two were in the van, two stood up in the barrow and two loaded the shells up. We used to have small anti-tank, fourteen-pound shells. These shells were put into green boxes. There were four into a green box .. and there was a screw at the top to hold them rigid. There were a hundred and twenty five to a lot, which was five hundred shells. The fifty six pounders were separate.'

Mrs Smith remembers enjoying singing during breaks, which recalled a health problem accentuated by her work, and working conditions generally:

'Because to get to the gatehouse you had to come through where we used to do our loading. And the sounds! you wouldn't need a microphone. The acoustics were very good, you see. So, we were all different types, so two used to sing high, two would sing harmony. But Miss

H

Cameron used to be the nurse there, and Miss Keeler, and she used to be quite amused. We used to harmonise to *The Last Rose of Summer*, and *Jingle, Jangle, Jingle*, and all the popular songs of the day. And, by an odd thing, I used to be bothered with a bad throat because I should have had my tonsils out and there was a family history of bleeding and my mother wouldn't let me go. But it was getting pretty much worse because the dust in the place was shocking. You see you only had narrow concrete paths, the rest was just black dust or brown dust. I used to have to go up to the medical room and get my throat painted with iodine, which was horrible. It was just a piece of stick and a piece of cotton wool but at that time we used to get fourteen Adexaline tablets every fortnight to keep our strength up, to complement the diet... And I went in and got my tonsils out. In on Monday, got my tonsils out on Tuesday and home on Wednesday. I was twenty years of age and it wasn't a pleasant thing, but it had to be done. And I got over it all right and went back to work.

'The Atlas Works. Well, I'll be honest, my heart used to sink when I opened the door. It was like cut out, a huge sliding door. And the heat! The light was never off because the place was blacked out. And when you opened the door the heat hit you because the furnaces were always warm. Well, at that time, they used to store guns there, off some of the big ships, huge guns and sometimes you had to hide behind there until they had the numbers up, so we would start and get our job done. But the work itself was very heavy, there's no doubt about that, for a nineteen year old. I've been so exhausted, sometimes I could hardly get on my coat, we had so much work on... You work two or three nights and worked a Sunday as well. You worked at a quarter to eight and I think you got three quarters of an hour for lunch, and that you got a break from half past five to six. And then you worked from six to a quarter to nine and in that ten minutes the night shift came on and they started at five to nine. Saturday was a half day, you stopped at dinner time on a Saturday and Sunday you worked, I think, to five or half past five.

'You wore a khaki overall and a khaki hat, not a dust cap, a nurse's, even a maid's, cap, and you had to have your hair tucked in, for the girls working the machinery. But the people were nice. At times people got word that so-and-so was killed. Eventually it happened to me. My boyfriend was killed. He was killed at twenty-two years of age. So that was the wedding off. Anyway, that's all in the past, but terrible at the time.'

Mary Tourish was a tailoress before the war. Her family were quite political, and she attended Socialist Sunday School as a young girl, which explains the political activities she alludes to. Noise is something most of our male interviewees, who began their training in their teens, take for granted when talking about their time in the railway works. For women however, beginning as adults and working there for a limited period, it was one of the most striking aspects of the working environment. Many, with hindsight, see war work as an important turning point in their lives. Mrs Tourish, however, remembers at the time that most people saw it as just another job, albeit in a somewhat unusual situation:

'We were on shifts days and nights alternately and I think we were on a twelve-hour shift if I remember correctly. I know the night-shift was a longer shift than the day-shift. You hadn't a clue what you were going into. And you went into the heat treatment with all the rivets, putting them out in all their sizes and everything and then you were gradually promoted to whatever job they decided. The pay varied. It was piece-work. We did the pieces for Sunderlands. It was Short Brothers that got it. We only did the flaps and the wings and the gun turrets you know. It was gey noisy, I'll tell you that!

'In saying that, you felt part of the war effort? No, I don't think so. It was just work, and that was it. Well, you knew it was for the war, but it didn't make such a great impression on you or most of them anyway. It was just a job. Well, you were aware of course that you were making aeroplanes and you were aware that there was a war on, but in the general sense I think they just accepted it was just another job. There was no-one unduly worried about the war. Now in saying that I'm not speaking for everyone because I was very conscious of the war, because previous to the war we had been out on a peace campaign and everything.'

Although women were always paid a lesser wage than men for working in the same workplace, and sometimes for doing the same job, comparatively speaking they often found themselves better off than they had been previously, which tended to take some of the sting from the obvious inequality. This was mainly because a woman's wage was held to be a complementary wage, if she was living at home with her parents or if she was married.

Margaret Burniston worked in Craigpark during the war, and illustrates her awareness of women's secondary position in the works, especially with regard to wages:

'We were always well paid, I mean although I say I started with twelve and fourpence, folks would start in Collins' with only six shillings. And we had no expenses, we walked to our work. When I became eighteen, that's when you got a standard wage.

'Men done different types of work making up the mixers and all the cables for the rubber and that. They had really dirty work, so there was always men in the place, but in war-time it didn't make any difference. I don't know what they done in munitions, I don't think the women were the same as the men even in munitions.'

Mary Williamson shows that, even though the rewards were

unevenly distributed, the atmosphere inside the works was made more egalitarian simply by the women's presence. Mary was disturbed by her initial experience on her first day inside Cowlairs, but she makes clear that a young, resilient personality could learn to prosper in her new environment, and make the best of the new social opportunities thrown up by her introduction into the workforce:

'I felt kind of strange because when I went in it was all boys and men that worked there. There was about two women as old as my mother and I was the youngest and I was only eighteen. And when I first went into the factory all the boys were shouting and bawling at me when you were passing. I felt really terrible the first day, I thought I could not stick it. In fact it was the first time I'd ever been in a factory. I'd never been in a factory before.

'I was put into the stores for the first two weeks to learn the machines —what a drill was and what a screwdriver was!—and things like that, before they put me out to work on the machines. I was a driller. I worked the drilling-machine 'til I was twenty-one, and then I went into the brass-finishing shop to work as a brass-finisher in there. It was a great atmosphere. The bosses didn't bother us as long as you did your work. But they didn't mix with us, they weren't hanging over your shoulder all the time. As long as your work got done that was fine.

'I worked twelve hours a day: eight in the morning to eight at night. I went in there at first when I was eighteen. My wages were nineteen shillings a week. And I got a rise when I was nineteen and a rise when I was twenty. To me that was great pay. 'Cause when I left the job before that, I was getting sixteen shillings, so I was still going higher again. When I turned twenty-one that was like your time was out, so I was getting apprentices' wages, and when I turned twenty-one my wages were about four pound a week. So that was quite a good jump in the wages you had.

'The men were really great. They were really grateful in every way. It was really good. See, I was in the youth hostels, so all the apprentices, well, not all the apprentices, but some of the apprentice boys and us girls went youth hostelling together. Went to ice-skating together and things like that. And dancing together. It really was good. They had wee concerts in the canteen during the dinner hour. Anybody that could sing or do anything went up to do it. I went up to sing, my name is Mary, "For it was Mary..."

'The apprenticeship lasted from when I was eighteen for three years and then I was in to the brass shop. And what I done in the brass shop was repair the windows. See, we repaired the locomotives in Cowlairs. So my job was repairing the windows and they brought the windows in when the hinges were stiff. We maybe had to put on new hinges or just get them working again, and then somebody would put the glass into them.

'We'd to leave Cowlairs. Left Cowlairs in December, 1945.'

Margaret Ingram demonstrates that chance could also work against you. An engineering works proved to be a purgatory for her, and her time in Springburn could be said to be even more regretable because she lost the liberty of a free choice. However, as with Alice and Joseph Amato, she did meet her husband there. Perhaps her distaste can also partly be explained by the fact that shell-producing entailed greater constrictions on individual behaviour, for obvious reasons, than some other aspects of warwork:

'I worked in the office in a paintworks in Dennistoun. And you were conscripted in actually. You got the choice, you either went to the land army, the forces or the munitions, and I didn't feel like going away from home, so I chose munitions. But the only problem was then they sent me to Springburn. Of course nobody wanted to go to Bishopton, it was like Siberia. It was quite a difference from working in an office to going into work in munitions but as I say you had no alternative. I never liked it at all. The only good thing that came out of it was that I met George. But my older sister went in there to work, she got in beside me. My other sister, she was too young, she was too young to get called up, but having my older sister beside me made it a wee bit better. But I never really liked it at all.

'I was on the heavier bay, the big shells. I don't know what size they were, I never really was that interested to find out. But first I worked a base-recessing machine that cut out the recess for putting the base plate down. Then I got a shift off that machine and onto a machine called a popping machine. It came from the lathe where they turned the shell, and there was still this piece of metal at the end and I sliced that off to go to the base recessors who finished the end of the shell.

'I was amongst the first girls that went in and the men that actually worked these machines taught us how to work them. Because I can always remember my first day in. The base recessor had a great big wheel that you turned to take the tool up to the shell. And the chap that was teaching me, he said, "Always remember to keep your face clear of that wheel." The first time I ever turned the wheel, I didn't keep my face clear enough. And it was a big metal spoke, just clattered. Swollen face my first day there.

'There was never any strikes amongst the girls. Never. They threatened them, some of the girls were in a union and they threatened strikes but they never came to anything. Women always had a lesser rate, by quite a bit. Exactly the same job!'

Margaret Sword's father was the leading charge-hand in Hyde Park works. With his aid, she became one of the most productive members of the newly-drafted in workforce, although this is not to underestimate her own contribution to this distinction. Her route to the works during the war reveals the undiscriminatory nature of induction into the war-effort. However undiscriminatory their induction, though, women were prevented from accumulating the same hours as men, even though they were paid at a lesser rate. What Mrs Sword does reveal is that women were granted certain small privileges for being in the works, privileges that were not granted to the men, which made the workplace a more humane environment. That these changes were welcome, such as improved washing facilities and another tea break in the afternoon, is shown by the fact that they became a permanent feature of most works after the war was over, and the women had left:

'I was in the first batch that was called up. All of us born in 1920 had to register then, you see. It came through on the radio and you had to go and register and that was you going to get called up. I went to work for the burner at first, and a few weeks after, Gourlay, the gaffer, told my father, "I want you to take Margaret." He coaxed him, he said, "Oh, well, if I've got to take her, I'll take her." He didn't like it because it put him in an awkward position. I was put onto this, what they called a 'Kitchen and Wade machine'. It's a very heavy-duty machine, it's an old machine. But none of them could touch Hyde Park for doing what they called the big copper super-heater tubes: that's for the tubes going into the engines. We used to have to bore them. I did all the firebox tube plates. I did some steel tube plates but it wasn't really my section, but I used to do it an odd time if they were busy. I did the butt straps. I think the butt straps go really to reinforce the engine at the side. They might have been fitted to reinforce the steam-engine.

'My father sharpened all my cutters. I used to hand-feed all my stuff and I could go through it quicker. The wee ones were all done with a tube drill. And then in the middle you had twenty-one of these holes. And if your cutter broke in the middle of this, you just had to stop your machine and get that out and chip away. My father would put in new cutters. You've got to make it that, you can't make the hole too big because you're working with a gauge. You've got to try it with what they call a male gauge. But the thing is, when that happens, you've got to make your cutter maybe just a hair bigger, so it'll clean out that hole and leave a nice clean hole.

'The man on the night-shift was that good at his job, he offered a hundred pounds to anybody who could do twenty-one big holes in the same time as him. He was the only one who could do it at that time. But the first time I did it my father says, "I'll go tell Mr Finlayson that he owes us a hundred pounds!" And he said, "Oh! You and Margaret are not counted on it." But it forced him to do more because he was working an hour more on the night-shift than I was.

'Then I used to do what they called the domes that sit on top of the engines. When you're boring the domes, the domes that come into you, they're shaped and you put them down and you bore them and then you tap them because they're screwed in with the screws at the top of the engine.

'I worked really hard in Hyde Park. I worked every day except a Saturday. A woman wasn't allowed to work on a Saturday because there were too many hours, we weren't allowed to work on a Saturday. You worked Monday, Tuesday, Wednesday, Thursday, Friday and Sunday. Monday and Wednesday and Friday were the days you worked to nine o'clock at night. That was from eight in the morning, you got a break in between, when the light went up you knew it was time for you to go for your tea. You went to this wee place to get your tea. And then you came back and just went on with your machine again. Then it came dinner-time, then in the afternoon you got a break. That was the women that got that break, not the men. Through the week you finished at half-past five, and then you went up the road, got your tea, and were back at six o'clock. Then you were ready to start the machine.

'But you worked really hard for your money. And no matter how you worked you couldn't get the same rate as a man. I was lower than a man. It was piece-work in those days. My father used to keep time for a lot of them. They were supposed to keep their own time, but my father would keep the time for some of them. My father used to come in at night and sit and write up books.

'You had to keep your hair under your hat because you could get scalped, putting your head down to look at a drill birling round so many revolutions to the minute. And if that drill caught even one hair!'

After both World Wars, women had to surrender their jobs to men, and the changes which followed the Second were more far reaching than those which followed the First. World War I had given rise to a number of social reforms—universal male suffrage, the vote for women over 30, free secondary schooling—which benefitted the whole of the country. The economic problems of the period limited the extent of change however, and further laid the path towards later decline. What can now be seen as the long term decline of Springburn's heavy industries began before 1914. The problems became acute once the postwar boom of 1919–21 had passed. Worldwide demand for locomotives slumped. Many countries were simply not able to afford them, while others began manufacturing their own, and protecting their industries with tariffs. In these circumstances, the Depression which followed the Wall Street Crash of 1929 had disastrous consequences and brought serious unemployment to the area. No solution to these problems was forthcoming from the NBL's directors; in 1936, one of them confidently predicted that the diesel would never replace the steam engine on main lines. The Depression was interpreted as another temporary cyclical slump which would pass. It was rearmament, though, not a revival in world trade, which saved the works from closure. Employment began to increase in 1937 and by 1940 Springburn experienced full employment. Pressure to produce vast quantities of war material took precedence over development of new technologies, and by 1945, Springburn was even further behind its competitors in Germany, America, and Japan. The worldwide shortages created by the war led to a temporary boom which petered out in the fifteen years after 1955. The 1939–45 war brought about more lasting change than 1914–18, nationally, as well as locally. These changes included improvements in working conditions, increased recognition of the role of trades unions and a wider acceptance of the philosophy of communal provision, which was an integral part of the working class culture of places like Springburn. Thus, at this moment of advance, the economic foundations on which it depended were already crumbling. The unresolved problems of heavy industry led to a steady decline from the mid-1950s onwards, bringing with it a deterioration in social conditions, and unprecedented levels of unemployment.

Women at milling machines during World War I.

A large Pattern Bomb manufactured in the Atlas Works in 1944.

Mrs Morrison and Bella Lyle at the North British Railway running sheds at Eastfield during World War I.

Cowlairs Works carriage cleaners, c1920. After 1918, women had to leave the works, except in unskilled areas such as cleaning.

Women using a Profile Oxy Acetelyne Cutting Machine in the Welding Shop, in Cowlairs, 1942. This machine is similar to that described by Maisie Gordon. Note the protective goggles, headscarf and dungarees she is wearing.

Fitters assistant working on a carriage bogie in Cowlairs in 1942. Her clogs were not just economical footwear: their wooden soles provided protection against sharp objects or heated rivets.

Tyre boring machine, Cowlairs 1942. Note the protective plastic eyeshield the operator is wearing.

Locomotive firebox. It was Margaret Sword's task to drill the boiler tube holes, on the right.

6

UNEMPLOYMENT

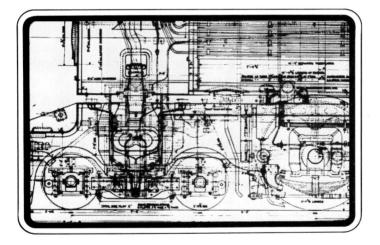

UNEMPLOYMENT

Unemployment involves the loss of everything that work means to people. Work is one of the most important ways of participating in society. It is a source of identity, and, of course, *the* determining factor in a standard of living. Unemployment means a person can no longer think of him or herself as contributing to society in a way that is expected of everyone. Instead, they are the recipient of what society judges to be the minimum needed to keep them alive.

Historically, unemployment was cyclical, following the booms and slumps of the trade cycle. However the underlying trend in Springburn's economic base has been one of decline since before the First World War. The North British Locomotive Company never manufactured as many engines again as it did in 1905, and St Rollox and Cowlairs were reduced to repair workshops soon after the amalgamation of 1923. Both the belief that slumps would be followed by booms, and the artificially high levels of demand during both World Wars and following the Second, concealed the deeper problems.

The delay in facing the changing circumstances made adapting to them more difficult when they could no longer be ignored. Springburn's recent trauma is all the more severe for its being unexpected, and because it involves a greater drop in standards than areas which suffered more in the past. According to one interviewee, an electric welder (who prefers to remain anonymous):

'Springburn was a district that was very lucky. We had a lot of works around Springburn and most locals at that time were working. But in other areas they had about eighty or ninety percent unemployment. We were very lucky here in Springburn, we had a lot of factories, a lot of works and you could get a job. If you were local you seemed to get priority.'

Henry Stewart, a carter and labourer, recalls the postwar boom, a time when many Springburn factories had workers doing 'two nights and a Sunday' overtime:

'You lived in Springburn and things were good at the war. And at the tail end of the war, rebuilding the city, and most of my pals are still joiners and plumbers and heating engineers and electricians and they've all worked most of the time, but funnily enough since recent years two or three of them have been unlucky enough and they have been out of work for quite a while.'

Until Glasgow District Council began moving people to new towns to relieve overcrowding in the late 1950s, there was a network alive in Springburn, cemented by work, bonding the community together. Work tied the individual to the family, the family to the community, and the community to the wider world. Springburn was an identifiable and important part of this wider world, which it served by its labour. Employment was a deep source of identity for both individuals and community. The network was supported by school and a myriad of church organisations. Unemployment damaged organic links at every level so that eventually the whole area and all its institutions were affected.

Springburn has never rediscovered this sense of identity, and the loss is palpable. Lack of confidence and fear of change are its depressing legacy.

While the idea that a skilled trade guaranteed a job for life was only partially true, it did mean that a person could realistically expect to exercise the same skill for life, and to work during the upturns in the economy. However it is easy looking back to forget the unplanned nature of many aspects of a person's life. With hindsight and the cushion of many years the path of a working life may appear smooth and almost predetermined, but this ignores the uncertainties and important decisions people have made, or that have been made for them. This makes any spell of unemployment a particularly revealing time in a person's life.

Finding work

Finding a job means, above all, being accepted as a responsible member of the community. Recruiting young workers was based on their belonging to a respectable family, known to be such either personally, by reputation, or simply by its head having a responsible job. John Dowie explains how he got a job as a cleaner in Eastfield Running Sheds:

'The set-up was, if you were a boy leaving school your father went into what they called the foreman and said he'd a boy leaving school in June. "Well, that's all right, just send him over." So the boy went over and he went into the foreman's office who just said, "Oh, right, aye, your father's a driver. Well, just write your name and your age on that bit of paper." And he had a look at it and said, "Right, you can start next week. You're a cleaner." That was how you got started.'

Before the school leaving age was raised, the first job a boy got was often very important in determining his 'prospects'. Some jobs were more sought after than others for this reason. In order to take the best candidates and to search for potential, the Co-op gave message boys a written test. William McGinley began in the Cowlairs Co-operative Society in this way and worked his way up to being a branch manager:

'There was so much unemployment in those days, if you got a job in the Co-op, at least it was a steady job, you know, so everybody was trying to get into it, so when there was applications, you had to go and sit a small exam, maybe about half-a-dozen boys or so sat for it.'

Jean Parker, a paper pattern maker and wages clerk with the Auxiliary Territorial Service, did not go job-hunting on her own, but with her mother, sharing ambitions—and interviews: 'When I left school, it was June 1940 and my mother went with me, we went down to Springburn to the employment exchange and they gave us jobs. But it was all shops like newsagents and things and I didn't want to work in a wee shop. When we went into the town, my mother came with me, and we went into the town to the employment exchange that used to be in Waterloo Street and they told us about this job in McDonalds' in Buchanan Street. So my mum and I toddled along and we saw a Mr Forbes, I can remember that big tall man, and he interviewed me and asked could I start on Monday, so I started on the Monday after I left school.'

Isobel Jordan got a job as a clerk in Braby's through a more indirect family connection:

'I had put my name in, I'd written to all the works round about. And it was a friend of my uncle's who worked in Braby's and told him there would be a vacancy. And she had spoken to the manager and I got the job. I was lucky. There was a bit of a depression and I wanted an office job. I had tried Hoey's our local drapers, but because I was left handed they wouldnae take me.'

Family ties were spread throughout the community and interacted with and reinforced other connections established through various voluntary organisations, especially those associated with churches. The Boys' Brigade and schools also provided contacts and recommendations. David Gould tells how he began his apprenticeship:

'I wasnae going to leave school. I was going to stay on because I hadnae a job. Just before I went back to school, one of the BB officers, a man called Bobby Sawyers, he came up to my house and started me, in a tannery firm, W & J Martin, Brunswick Street, in the office. The tannery was in Bridgeton. I started in there, working there a year before I served my time.'

Jobs were thus allocated as much on who a person was as on individual merit, and for those outside the traditional networks, entry was extremely difficult. Breaking into areas of relative privilege and exclusivity such as apprenticeships, except at boom times, required someone to 'speak for you'. The local connections were also convenient for employers, as they reinforced workplace discipline. For people within the community, the ties provided a certain amount of protection against the threat of unemployment to the income of the family as a whole, some sense of control over the jobs market. The existence of this permanent threat also placed a special value on jobs which were seen to be secure. Alec MacGregor, whose father was a policeman, expressed it in this way:

'In 1947, you know, the job was worth how long it lasted. If you got into the police or insurance or banking, you knew that would last you the rest of your life. So a joiner on the railway wasnae paid like a joiner outside, because the joiner outside got a different job every six weeks, but the joiner on the railway was there for the rest of his life. But he was paid less than the joiner outside.'

Youth unemployment

People were vulnerable to unemployment during periods of depression, at particular times in their lives, for example when leaving school, at the age of sixteen, and on completing apprenticeship. (In many jobs women were expected to leave when they got married. This was usually not considered being made unemployed.) Fred Holmes recalls such an early experience of being laid off, purely because of his age:

'I was idle at the time when I was sixteen. It was the common thing, when you turned sixteen if you were a message boy you got the sack. At that age the employers had to put stamps on their card, you know, health insurance and unemployment stamps. Rather than bother paying extra you just got the sack. But the riot was really on. At that time you went when you were sixteen to get any benefit at all. I think it was seven shillings, and you'd to attend a half-day at the school, five days of the week. If you missed a day you got a shilling off your cash, if you were being paid, you know.'

Cathy McIlroy, who worked both in Cowlairs and on trams during the war, recalls how her brother was a victim of the exploitation of the apprenticeship system: 'I had a brother unemployed. Was it a five-year apprenticeship that was served at Cowlairs? Anyway, what they called their time was out and they were no longer an apprentice. They were a journeyman and their wages automatically jumped up. Well, they got their books because that was them capable of doing a man's job. And they didn't need it because they could find another apprentice. I mind my brother being idle. He was idle for a long time.'

Skilled and unskilled

Skilled men were in general much more mobile than unskilled, in good times able to change jobs to get better rates of pay, and in hard times moving to where there were jobs. Further, except in the most severe depressions, the factories kept on a core of skilled workers, to give themselves a base to build on when things improved. Joseph Docherty, for example, had an extremely varied career:

'I served my time, 1940 to 1944, and then I went into the army, out the Caley. And when I came out the army, I didn't go back to the railway for a couple of years, then I went to the running sheds at Corkerhill, and I was about five years there. And I left there, just started jogging about and then after a while I started on night shift at NB Loco. Quite a lot of people left, and you'd go somewhere else where the piecework was OK, and then you'd come back when another started, because the first two or three, you didn't make any money out of them, you know. And while I was on the nightshift it was beginning to peter out, the order was about completed, and I heard that GEC were starting people over in the Atlas works, for a big order of electric locks. So I went over there and they gave me a job. So I worked with them until that order was completed and then the NB offered me a job back, doing their diesel engines. Putting in the diesel and the Voith gearbox for the Indian order. So I worked until it was finished and then of course the NB was in its death throes and I left. And a few years later I went back again. They had shut quite a bit of it down, but they were making diesel engines for British Railways, diesel locomotives like. I was in the fabricating shop there making the actual diesel engines, you know. So all in all, I did jump about a bit. It was quite common that. I dare say there was a hard core of NB guys right enough, but blokes like myself went in and out.'

In depressed times skilled workers would take unskilled jobs when they could get them. In Fred Holmes' case this provided a sharp experience of the width of the divide between the two categories. He was 'an experienced machine worker who'd been in charge of sixteen girls but could not get work in Springburn. So I was idle for three weeks. At that time I just called into the Labour Exchange to collect my cash, my money, which I paid for, and after three weeks I got a green card to go down to Cowlairs works for a job. The manager asked me what I'd done before, I told him I'd been in charge of sixteen machines. He says "you can't expect to get that sort of job." And here listen, I didnae expect that because you couldnae get on a machine unless he said so. So I got a job in Cowlairs works just sweeping the floor and so on, odd jobs that the men on the machines treated you as though you were a lower class of being.'

Being paid off

The word 'redundancy' has acquired its powerful connotations relatively recently, and it is interesting that it is usually the workers rather than the jobs which are described as being 'redundant'. In its colloquial usage, it also refers to a severance payment, often an amount much larger than the statutory requirement, negotiated by the unions. Until the 1960s, workers frequently got no notice of being paid off and no payment other than a week or a month in lieu of notice (this was to pre-empt vandalism by the workers). Fred Holmes had a particularly harrowing experience of sudden redundancy: 'I had been working for a firm in the Southside; outside work, doing it outside the work. The morning I got married I got my books. Just like that. No more work. And I couldn't tell my wife I had no job to come back to from Bangor when we went on our honeymoon. Well, there we were. So we had to live on one pound and thirteen pence a week, the two of us. Pay our own bills, the rent and rates and all that. But it meant that we had no cash, no cash for spare clothes or pictures or anything of that sort, you know... From the time I got married for two and a half years running I was actually idle.'

One of today's problems for people over 50 who are made redundant is the obsolescence of their skills and the prejudice of employers against older workers. Many cannot expect ever to work again and face a prolonged retirement without the support of the community in which they grew up. This problem is new only in terms of its scale. Martha MacMillan's high level of skill enabled her to find a new job, but it is noteworthy that her trade—she made tracings of technical drawings for use on the shop floor—no longer exists. She recalls:

'Even in the 1960's, people of 45 and over found it difficult to get work ... In 1961 the NB was closing down and actually the year before they closed they were paying off some of the tracers, so unfortunately I was one of them. I got paid off and my niece was paid off too, we were both paid off at the same time. And I thought, "Well, I'm 51 years of age, I'll never get a job." Rene was only twenty-eight and she was engaged to be married, she wasn't worrying the same. Anyway, I spoke to the works manager who was Mr Alec MacDonald. I said "I've written to Singers in Clydebank and could I use your name as a reference?" He said, "Certainly." So I did that. Then Murray Rose, who's my niece's husband now, he had tried to get Rene into the office at Stevens but they wouldn't take her in because she was engaged to be married. So he said to Rene, "Tell your aunt Martha to write in, she'll maybe get a chance." So I wrote in and I got two letters, one from Singers, one from Stevens, both came the same day. The same day was the interviews, one in the morning, the other in the afternoon. So I went to Singers and I practically accepted the job and I phoned Stevens and told them that I had got an offer of a job, and she said she would like me to come and see her. So in the interval I went back to the Hyde Park offices to get Mr MacDonald and I told him the position. He said, "Well, Martha, if you're getting the chance in Stevens I would take it, you're not getting all that travelling to Singers." See, I was thinking the train at the station is round from where I stay, but as he said, it's mobbed at night and the morning too with workmen. Anyway, I went over to Stevens and got my interview and I had a very good interview. So anyway I said to her, "I can't accept until I see Mr MacDonald because I told him the position and he had spoken for me." And in the interval I contacted Mr MacDonald and he said to me "Take Stevens", and I started on the Monday morning there.'

Unemployment relief and the means test

Most comments on unemployment before the last war are based around memories of the harsh application of the rules for the receipt of financial help from the government. These were complicated and changed with each government, but most workers relied on their payments from their National Insurance contributions, established in 1911. Once these ran out there were a variety of national and local schemes including the Poor Law, or 'the Parish', which was abolished in 1929. Martha MacMillan recalls that when her father was idle:

'It was terrible because he was the mainstay. You know what he got for me? He was idle when I left school, he got two shillings a week to keep me. And he only got it on the understanding that I wouldn't be working during the holidays. Well, I was only three weeks off on holiday when I got my job. I wrote into the papers for it and I got it because of the nice letter that I'd sent in. That's what my boss told me. He said between the nice paper I'd used and the way I'd phrased my letter was the way I'd got the job. I didn't know anybody in the place, you know. And they'd the cheek to claim back six shillings for my father on his next pay at the buroo. My father says, "What's this for?", and he says, "Oh, well, your daughter's started work". "Look," he says, "I had to keep her for those three weeks." Now that's a fact... There wasn't any DHSS, it was a case of this: my mother was desperate when father was what they termed on the 'gap', and they should never have put him on the 'gap' with a family like what he had. It means a gap of money: you got no money for maybe a fortnight. What do you live on? There was no work and no money. The money was scarce and they were dividing it out sort of way, but where it was a needy case they looked over that, you see. Well, my mother told my father straight, "If you don't go," (there was the Parish in those days), "I'm going." So father wouldnae have my mother going, father was very proud, you see, and he finally had to go. And they sent him back to the bureau to tell them that he should never have been on the 'gap'. That was their words. Sent him up to go and get his money. The children got at that time two shillings a head. Even in those days two shillings didn't go very far.'

The most bitter memories of all are associated with the Means Test, introduced along with other measures after the financial crisis of 1931. This limited unemployment benefit which could be drawn as of right to a maximum of twenty-six weeks. Over fifty years later, questions about unemployment inevitably raise memories of the extra humiliations the Means Test added to any man's failure to fulfil his traditional responsibilities as provider for his family. Of course, the interviews are contemporary, but when the man himself wasn't here to comment, his surviving family's distress is only too apparent. This is in part due to the fact that many of those subjected to scrutiny in their own homes were skilled workers experiencing such an intrusion for the first time. Relief from the Labour Exchange based on National Insurance contributions had no stigma, but the Means Test was applied in a manner very similar (and sometimes by the same people) to the way the old Poor Law regulations had been administered.

John Craig, an apprentice fitter in St Rollox in the early 1930s, recalls the brutal nature of one aspect of the Test, and his father's response to the indignity of it:

'You had this problem with the Means Test. You got so much off the labour exchange, but they kept control, and following you about would come up to your house. Mother had a lovely big organ in the house. He says, "Well, you don't get any more money for four weeks until you sell that organ." And my father belted him down the stairs. He never came back again. But anything you had that wasn't actually for use, the likes of cookers, they couldn't touch cookers, utensils, carpets, ordinary furniture. But anything that was regarded as something you didn't require, you had to sell that or else you didn't get any money.'

Benefit could be reduced if there was a son or daughter working or if there was a pensioner living. The consequences were that as, Margaret Burniston recalls, 'if any of them were working in the house they actually had to leave the house.' Even quite young boys had to leave home, and, at a time when young people usually lived with their parents until they got married, this was viewed as breaking up the family.

The politics of unemployment

Before the First World War, to speak of the politics of unemployment would not have been a meaningful phrase, because for most people the condition was only temporary and the problems were economic, not political. State-subsidised benefits for the unemployed had been introduced three years prior to the beginning of the First World War, but these treated the symptoms, not the causes. After the war, though, as the prolonged slump of the 1920s worsened into the depression of the 1930s, unemployment became for many people a fact of life. The Communist Party at this time as a relatively new party for whom politics and economics were inseparable. They were hungry for engagement in issues which surrounded working-class life, and gave themselves a national profile by stressing their leadership of the National Unemployed Worker's Movement, a movement that had cross-party support. This gave them the opportunity not only to underline their politics but also to demonstrate a common-sense pragmatism in assisting people attempting to claim benefits. Joseph Sweeney was an ex-soldier who had been wounded in the war. He was unemployed and blacklisted for most of the 1920s. A Communist Party member, he organised the

Springburn Branch of the National Unemployed Worker's Movement. His wife was treasurer, and their family grew up in a household environment that reflected the parents' political commitment. Joseph Sweeney's daughter, Cathy Craig, told us of her father's work and in particular about the Communist Party's attempts to provide leadership for the unemployed:

'The Labour Party at that time didn't have much to do with the unemployed. The Labour Party saw themselves as of the organised workers within the trade union movement and that sort of thing, the employed. And the Labour Party didn't organise the unemployed at all, whereas the Communist Party realised that these workers had to be organised. There was nowhere they would fit in, they couldn't be members of the trade union movement because they weren't organised in that. And the Communist Party obviously saw this need and they instituted the National Unemployed Workers Movement, and this was an all-embracing thing.

'Before they actually had the Means Test as such, they used to come along and investigate what their financial arrangements were. Who was in the house, what means of support they had, and all this sort of thing, and in some cases you had to trace how old people were, how long they had worked, and how long they'd been in the country and all that sort of thing. And the National Unemployed Workers' Movement —my father saw the need—what they needed at that time were people who could make themselves acquainted with the laws, to make themselves acquainted with the legal arguments that were going to be used about cutting people's benefit, which was little enough as it was then. And they used to have to go to a Court of Referees, would you believe, along at the Labour Exchange and they would decide whether their benefit would be cut or whether they actually qualified for benefit.

'And then of course you had the sort of itinerant workers, which was very difficult, and I mean all this sort of thing had to be sorted out and as I say, apart from this once, the Means Test was applied. That was a tragic business because this meant that lads had to leave home, because while they were staying at home their father's benefit had to cover them. They didn't get full benefit, and they used to get, what was it, roughly fifteen shillings a man got to look after his family. And you got two shillings per child. And you can imagine a family trying to live! And if a chap, if a lad happened to get work, and a lot of the lads at that time used to go pick potatoes, but I mean there just wasn't any work. I mean it's bad enough now, but I mean there was just no work. And they used to go out and get the odd day, and you were supposed to tell them exactly how much they got for that odd day picking potatoes, and that was deducted from the money that the father would get. And if they were found out cheating, as they said it was, then the father's money would be taken away completely and he'd have to go up and get subsistence money and the tragedy, the suicides, the things that happened. I mean families breaking up, boys would leave home, they wouldn't know where to go, but they felt they were just a burden on their parents.

'My father was the one who set up in Springburn this group of them, who were astute enough, shall we put it like that, to be able to counteract the arguments which were used against people. Because if you've got someone, I didn't mean to be derogatory when I was talking about semi-literate people, but if you've got someone who's faced with a form who doesn't write, and he's frightened to death of officialdom, because people bring out these official looking forms, it makes their minds go numb. I mean not that they're stupid by any manner of means, but they've never been taught how to write or how to counter arguments and how to realise that they've got rights, as it were. And the NUWM set themselves up as this, and it was a fantastic job because they were practically lawyers. I mean they trained themselves so that they knew exactly what the law was, how it could be applied, and they used to go up and it was a sort of battle of wits over a number of them, in the Court of Referees.'

Unemployment in Springburn today

Springburn today has an unemployment rate of 27%, and nearly half of that number have been out of work for over a year. What this means was summarised in an official report on the social and economic costs of the closure of British Rail Engineering Ltd (formerly St Rollox), the last of Springburn's railway factories, with 1600 redudancies:

'Unemployment is not only a waste of potential resources and a major factor contributing to social unrest, but also is associated with both a deterioration in the health of communities affected over a long period and with an increase in the crime rate. Any rise in crime or the incidence of illness, whether mental or physical, also affects public expenditure, particularly government spending on prisons, the police, law courts and the Health Service and the use of various social services. It is however not possible to estimate these costs.' (Glasgow District Council Planning Department, 1985, paragraph 6.2)

Though the closure of BREL may be seen as the working out of the process of decline which began before 1914 and of centralisation in England which began in 1923, the social consequences have both important similarities and differences with the earlier periods of unemployment. The feeling of community, once so strong in Springburn, as in many similar industrial areas, has been undermined by developments which include local government units, the spread of the mass media and of an international youth culture. However it is arguable that high unemployment is the single most important factor in eroding the connections between the individual, school, family and community. The social networks of parents and grandparents, and their traditional wisdom based on apprenticeships in large works and a belief in secure jobs for life, do not help young people function in today's labour market. Unemployment also damages motivation to achieve in school, as good results and good behaviour are no longer automatically rewarded with a improved job prospects. The cutting of communal ties means that unemployment is a much more solitary experience than was common in the 1930s. The relatively low income at that period even for skilled people in work meant that it was essentially a non-materialistic culture, in which social meaning was expressed through participation in organisations ranging from cycling clubs to friendly societies and from Socialist Sunday Schools to the Boys' Brigade. The immense growth in material prosperity since 1945, and the exercise of consumer purchasing power as the main way of participating in society, further isolates the unemployed, both individually and collectively. Reincorporating them into the rest of the community is the most important challenge facing Springburn in the next decade.

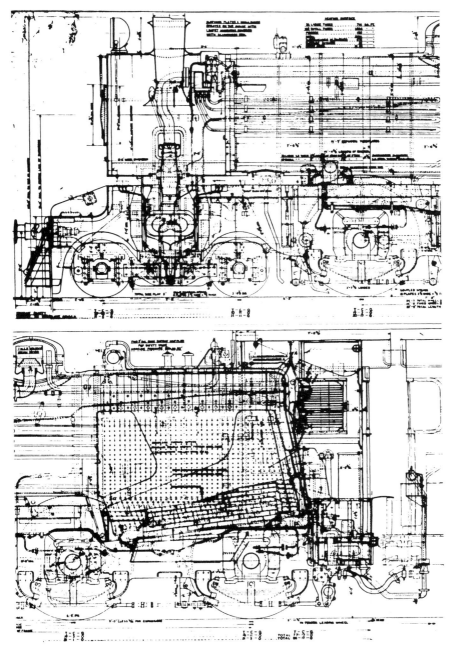

The last tracing Martha MacMillan made in the Hyde Park works before being made redundant.

WORK IN THE 80s

Andy Davis of E Mulligan, Coal Merchants, Pinkston Road.

Khalid Siddiq, CVC Videovision, Springburn Way.

Brian McGeough, 'Angela's' fruit and vegetable van, Balgrayhill Road.

Stan Brown, Pathology (Special Techniques), Stobhill.

Charles Hughes, Cape Boards production worker.

Mary Muirhead, Anna Redmond, May Porteous, Gillies Graham and Mr R Graham MPS, staff of Anderson & Ireland 1988.

Helen Camley, Domestic Staff, Stobhill.

Edna Walker, Blindcraft bedding department.

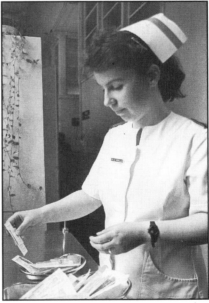

Fireman Tom Scott wearing Fire Brigade breathing apparatus, Springburn Fire Station, Midton Street.

Ann McCallum, Enrolled Nurse, Stobhill General Hospital, Balornock Road.

Ann Graham, travel agent, Diaper Travel.

Police Constables Robert Fitzpatrick and David King with Mrs Betty Kerr, janitor, Bonnybroom Nursery, Balornock.

John Davidson, Glasgow District Council Cleansing Department.

Marie Hinton, Fish Department Supervisor, Presto Supermarket, Springburn Shopping Centre.